The Bahai Movement

Also from Westphalia Press
westphaliapress.org

The Idea of the Digital University

Dialogue in the Roman-Greco World

The History of Photography

International or Local Ownership?: Security Sector Development in Post-Independent Kosovo

Lankes, His Woodcut Bookplates

Opportunity and Horatio Alger

The Role of Theory in Policy Analysis

The Little Confectioner

Non Profit Organizations and Disaster

The Idea of Neoliberalism: The Emperor Has Threadbare Contemporary Clothes

Social Satire and the Modern Novel

Ukraine vs. Russia: Revolution, Democracy and War: Selected Articles and Blogs, 2010-2016

James Martineau and Rebuilding Theology

A Strategy for Implementing the Reconciliation Process

Issues in Maritime Cyber Security

Understanding Art

Homeopathy

Fishing the Florida Keys

Iran: Who Is Really In Charge?

Contracting, Logistics, Reverse Logistics: The Project, Program and Portfolio Approach

The Thomas Starr King Dispute

Springfield: The Novel

Lariats and Lassos

Mr. Garfield of Ohio

The French Foreign Legion

War in Syria

Ongoing Issues in Georgian Policy and Public Administration

Growing Inequality: Bridging Complex Systems, Population Health and Health Disparities

Designing, Adapting, Strategizing in Online Education

Gunboat and Gun-runner

Pacific Hurtgen: The American Army in Northern Luzon, 1945

Natural Gas as an Instrument of Russian State Power

New Frontiers in Criminology

Feeding the Global South

The Bahai Movement

A Series of Nineteen Papers

by Charles Mason Remey

WESTPHALIA PRESS
An Imprint of Policy Studies Organization

The Bahai Movement: A Series of Nineteen Papers
All Rights Reserved © 2017 by Policy Studies Organization

Westphalia Press
An imprint of Policy Studies Organization
1527 New Hampshire Ave., NW
Washington, D.C. 20036
info@ipsonet.org

ISBN-13: 978-1-63391-590-9
ISBN-10: 1-63391-590-5

Cover design by Jeffrey Barnes:
jbarnesbook.design

Daniel Gutierrez-Sandoval, Executive Director
PSO and Westphalia Press

Updated material and comments on this edition
can be found at the Westphalia Press website:
www.westphaliapress.org

The Bahai Movement

A Series of Nineteen Papers

BY
CHARLES MASON REMEY

Published in the Ninety-fifth Year after
the Birth of Baha'o'llah

Second Edition

PRESS OF
J. D. MILANS & SONS
WASHINGTON, D. C.

PREFACE

THESE papers treating of the Bahai Movement have been written at various times and places during the past two years, some typewritten copies of which have been circulated among people interested in the work. Because of the growing interest in the Bahai Cause and the increasing demand for literature upon the subject, it now seems advisable to publish these articles in book form, in the hope that they may be of service to those who desire more knowledge of the Bahai teaching.

C. M. R.

21 March, 1912,
Washington, D. C.

In the Persian and Arabic languages each letter has a numerical value and each name or word has as its numerical value the sum of the values of its component letters. A=1, B=2, H=5. Thus 9 is the numerical value of the name Baha, and this number, which is the greatest of simple numbers, is used by the Bahais as a symbol of the name.

TABLE OF CONTENTS

	Page
I. INTRODUCTION	1
II. THE BAB	6
III. BAHA'O'LLAH	14
IV. ABDUL-BAHA	25
V. THE MANIFESTATION OF THE WORD OF GOD	35
VI. RELATION OF THE BAHAI MOVEMENT TO THE RELIGIONS OF THE PAST	42
1. CHRISTIANITY	43
2. JUDAISM	45
3. ISLAM	47
4. ZOROASTRIANISM	49
5. HINDUISM	51
6. BUDDHISM	53
7. MODERN THOUGHT	55
RESUMÉ	57
VII. THE BAHAI SACRED WRITINGS	59
VIII. SOCIAL REFORMS, LAWS AND ORDINANCES	64
IX. THE NEED OF THE TIMES	72
X. ORIENTAL-OCCIDENTAL UNITY	76
XI. ETERNAL LIFE	80
XII. HEAVEN AND HELL	83
XIII. SCIENCE AND RELIGION	88
XIV. THE SUPERNATURAL	90
XV. EDUCATIONAL ASPECT OF THE BAHAI TEACHING	91
XVI. THE BAHAI MOVEMENT AND THE ECONOMIC QUESTIONS OF THE DAY	94
XVII. THE EVOLUTION OF MAN	96
XVIII. THE METHOD OF TEACHING AND THE GROWTH OF THE BAHAI MOVEMENT	98
XIX. A PERSONAL TESTIMONY	103

I.
INTRODUCTION

At the present time the religious world is in a state of change. It has broken away from the cold and hard creed and dogma of the past, and it is awakening to, and reaching out for, a broader conception of truth—*the universal religion*. This, the universal religion, is what The Bahai Movement offers to the world.

While there are many philosophies, (religion, because of man's limitations, has taken upon itself many and varying forms of thought) from the spiritual view-point there is but one religion. There is but one God and there is but *one* spiritual relation between HIM and the individual souls of men. The knowledge of the spiritual relation between the Creator and the created is the one only and true religion. It is the basic principle of all religious systems, and, shorn of the superstitions and imaginations of the past, it will be the religion of the future.

Through knowing, understanding and living the principles of The Kingdom, men will become united; the various religions, sects, and cults will cease to exist as such, and all men will live as brothers. The Bahai Movement is actually bringing about this milennial condition. Through its teaching and influence the spiritual limitations of an undeveloped humanity are disappearing, and the Truth, which is the love of God, is manifesting itself here on this earth as brotherhood among men.

This present day is characterized by a great spiritual awakening, the like of which has never before been in the world. This awakening is manifest among all people, in all countries, and under all conditions. During the past sixty-five years the world has entered upon a new spiritual era: people who have made a study of the religious work of today realize this fact, notwithstanding their own personal view-points. In the Christian world we see the effect of this awakening in so convincing a manner that illustrations are unnecessary. In the other religions the same is clearly and strikingly visible in the many changes and movements which, in these latter years have characterized Judaism, Islam, Hinduism and Buddhism. This spiritual awakening is universal. It manifests itself differently under varying conditions, social, racial and religious, but considered as a whole, it indicates that now the soul of the world is awake and searching, and that nothing short of the universal truth will appease its hunger and quench its thirst. It is this universal soul-need which the Bahai teaching is meeting and satisfying.

The teachers and prophets, the founders of the world-religions, have been seers as well as channels of truth to the people of their days. Through spiritual understanding and wisdom, they foresaw this latter-day universal awakening and demand for truth. They also foresaw the supply for this demand in the coming of another channel of divine grace, the Latter-Day Messiah. This, the greatest of all manifestations, they prophesied would arise with spiritual understanding and power, reveal and demonstrate the universal truth, which exists in all religions, and unite all men and establish the universal religion, the Kingdom of God on earth. That this manifestation, the greatest of all GOD'S Messengers, *has come* is the message that the Bahai Movement is giving to the world.

There was a time when the religions of the world were considered as isolated and separate one from another, with no connection whatever; but now, in the light of this new teaching, all are seen to have emanated from the one source—which is GOD. As parts of one great body, they are organically connected. Each has been a step leading humanity to a higher conception of the Creator and preparing souls for the time when all men would unite, worshipping HIM in spirit and in truth. Thus one prophet appeared, building upon the foundation of His predecessors, fulfilling their prophecies and accomplishing the hopes of their followers by leading humanity on, a stage further, in soul development. Each prophet prepared the way for the coming of the succeeding prophetic dispensation. In this way have all religious movements of the past been integral parts of the foundation of God's Kingdom here on earth, whose completed structure *now is appearing in the Revelation of Baha'o'llah, in which the prophecies, hopes and fruits of all religions are realized.*

The Bahai Movement offers to the world a teaching applicable to the modern needs of humanity. It offers religion renewed. All truth emanates from "The Word of God" and through GOD'S mouth-pieces, His anointed ones, it comes into the world for the soul-quickening of humanity. The teachings of all religions in their beginning were pure but, as time passed, man-created philosophy and thought crept in killing the pure spirit of truth until, finally, little remained save creed, dogma and ceremony. So, a purer conception of truth being needed, another divine revelation appeared. Today the creeds and dogmas of the past are without spiritual potency. A new spiritual quickening is necessary, and, as of old, GOD has again revealed His Word, that all men, of all nations and of all races, may receive more abundantly than ever before, His spirit. This He has accomplished through the three inspired leaders of the Bahai Movement; through The Bab, who was the herald and the First Point of this Revelation; through Baha'o'llah, who was the revealer of The Word; and now through Abdul-Baha, who is the expounder of The Word, in whom all things are fulfilled.

Going back to the dawn of history one finds the family to be the unit of civilization. Later on, many families are found uniting under a patriarch, forming a clan or tribe. Still later are found federations of clans or tribes, from which nations have come into existence. Now the next step is the absorbing of all nations and races into one great world people. This is the order of the progress of mankind, and in the fruit of the teachings of Baha'o'llah is seen the beginning of this great end. Civilization is the product of religion. Each of the world's civilizations had its birth in a religious movement. Civilization has always been the fruit of the spiritual awakening of a people who, by political and geographical barriers, were isolated from external influences. In this day geographic, political and social barriers have, through travel and communication, been obliterated until now man is limited only by the confines of this planet. We are on the threshold of an universal epoch. That which affects one people politically, socially or financially, affects the whole world, and the great universal civilization so rapidly advancing is casting its signs before. In the Bahai teaching *is* the spiritual power to unite men's souls. It is forming a spiritual nucleus from which will spring the universal civilization to be, of the magnitude of which we can now form no conception

Today, has begun a new order of things upon the earth. Mankind is attaining spiritual maturity, and is demanding more spiritual food than the old forms and dogmas of religion can give him. Through spiritual enlightenment, ignorance is being dispelled, causing a change of soul—a change in man's nature—and this change is being felt the world round. The mission and object of the Bahai Movement is the uniting of men of all nations, religions and races in the love of GOD and the brotherhood of man. Its teaching is constructive. It fulfills the highest hopes of the religions of the past, and is uniting all men in the great universal religion of the future.

II.
THE BAB.

Mirza Ali Mohammed, known as The Bab,* was born in October, 1819, in the city of Shiraz, in southern Persia. His father, a Seyed or descendant of the prophet Mohammed, died during his infancy, whereupon the young child was adopted into the family of an uncle, a man of virtue, who reared Him, giving Him such elementary education in the Persian language as was customary among the sons of the merchant class to which He belonged. On attaining maturity Mirza Ali Mohammed went into business with His uncle and was for some time located in Bushire upon the Persian Gulf. As a young man He was noted for purity, gentleness, and charm. Even those who afterwards opposed and persecuted Him and His followers so cruelly, never attacked His personal character. Much religious meditation, they claimed, had unbalanced His mind.

On May 23d, 1844, moved by the Spirit of God, Mirza Ali Mohammed gave His teachings to the world. At that time from various parts of Persia, were gathered together in Shiraz eighteen prepared souls, men of wisdom to whom it had been given to understand spiritual realities, and to these chosen disciples Mirza Ali Mohammed revealed His mission. He was the door ("Bab") or forerunner of a great prophet and teacher soon to appear. He, The Bäb, had been divinely sent as a herald to warn the people of the coming of The Promised One and to exhort them to purify themselves and prepare for His advent. One—whom He entitled "He whom God

---
*"Bab" is the Arabic and Persian word for door or gate.

shall manifest," the Latter-Day Messiah, promised in all the revealed writings of the past—was soon to come and establish The Kingdom of God upon earth.

These eighteen first disciples of The Bab were known as "The Letters of The Living". They, with Himself as "The Point," formed the nucleus for the dissemination of the new teaching. As soon as The Bab had instructed these disciples in His simple doctrines, He sent them into various parts of Persia with the commission to teach and to proclaim His appearance. He then, with one of His followers, went upon the annual pilgrimage to Mecca where, before a concourse of over one hundred thousand pilgrims assembled from all parts of the Moslem world. He made His first public declaration. When He returned to Bushire, His cause was known in many parts of the country, and was so rapidly gaining adherents that the members of the Mussulman clergy became alarmed lest through the rise of this new cult they might lose their hold over the people. Then were The Bäb's travels, teachings, and trials increased.

From Bushire The Bab went to Shiraz where He was roughly treated by the Moslems, placed under guard and ordered to remain within the confines of His house. There, nevertheless, many had access to Him, were attracted, and believed in His teaching, men of prominence and learning as well as those of the more humble walks of life. The world about him was against Him, yet through the power of Divine Love He overcame all obstacles and won the hearts of the people.

The Bab next journeyed to Esphahan, where by that time He had many followers. There He was received by the governor of the city, a

Christian, who openly acknowledged belief in Him and befriended Him in many ways, giving Him facilities for meeting and teaching the people. This aroused the anger of the clergy to such a degree that the priests sought to put The Bab to death. Then it was that the governor concealed Him in the official quarters where He remained for some time in safety.

The friendly governor dying suddenly, and The Bab's whereabouts becoming known, an order was issued by the government in Teheran for Him to be conveyed thither. Accordingly, under guard He proceeded toward the capital. In the cities and villages along the route of travel His message had preceded Him, and wherever He went he found eager listeners and seekers whose souls He won. Even His captors could not resist the spirit which flowed from Him, and many of them became His friends and staunch supporters.

The ministers of state being informed of the rapid growth of the Babi Movement and fearing lest The Bab's presence in Teheran would agitate the clergy and possibly produce a religious uprising, another order was issued to the effect that He should not approach the city but tarry in a town not far distant. From there He was soon removed to the fortress of Maku in the extreme northwestern part of Persia. On this long, cross-country journey. The Bab passed through many cities and, as always, His fame spread widely, and many believed and followed in His path.

Among the most prominent of The Bab's followers was Kurratu l'Ayn, poet, orator and heroine of the cause, who, after an eventful career in which she stood forth as a powerful exponent of the new faith, suffered a martyr's death. As a woman many decades ahead of her time, her life and example are an inspiration to all, and especially to her sisters of the Orient who, through the cause for which she died, are now being lifted from their former condition of ignorance and oppression into one of knowledge and freedom.

As one listens to the accounts of the lives of the early Babis, (The Bab's adherents were known as Babis) of their missions and labors, sufferings and martrydoms, he sees the wonderful spirit of the love of God which actuated them as they responded to the call. One is thrilled as he realizes that the days of a vital and a burning faith, such as moved the apostles and fathers of old, have again come to pass, for this latter-day religion is bearing the same manner of spiritual fruit as the religions of the past bore in their earlier days.

The daily increase in the numbers of The Bab's followers caused the Persian authorities to remove Him from Maku to a more remote imprisonment in the castle of Chih-rik, where He could be more closely guarded and would be less likely to communicate with the outside world. At length, His following having attained to great proportions, the clergy became thoroughly alarmed and instigated a heresy trial or public examination of His doctrines. This investigation was held in Tabriz by the authority of the governor of the province, and before the tribunal The Bab was brought a prisoner. All manner of insults and indignities were heaped upon Him, and finally He was flogged, one of the chief mullahs applying the rods with his own hands. After this The Bab was returned to his former prison in the fortress of Chih-rik.

About this time began the early persecutions

and massacres of the Babis in Persia. Aroused by their priests, the fanatical Moslems fell upon the believers in many parts of the land, pillaging and burning their homes, and torturing and murdering men, women and children. These crimes are too revolting to be mentioned in detail. The heart seems to stand still when listening to the accounts of the marvelous courage and fortitude of even the children, not to mention that of the women and men. These souls with the greatest calmness and joy submitted to the most fiendish tortures and death rather than recant, or deny their faith, when denial would have saved them. One's heart beats rapidly when he realizes that through this suffering these martyrs were lighting the way that people might be prepared to meet the One promised to appear and establish The Kingdom upon earth.

Sometimes Babi fugitives banded themselves together to resist the attacks of the Moslems, and in some instances they defended themselves bravely only to be slaughtered in the end by the overwhelming number of their adversaries. That "the blood of the martyrs is the seed of the church" is again proven to the world, for with the shedding of each drop of Babi blood the cause gained numbers of adherents. People who knew little or nothing of The Bab and His teachings, save that a great prophet's forerunner had come, were confirmed in the faith and went forth to serve, and to die when called upon.

Islam is the state religion of Persia, therefore that which shakes its power produces a like effect in the workings of the government. At length, seeing the cause to be steadily on the increase, the prime minister of the state ordered that The Bab be killed, hoping thus to put an end to the matter and to place himself in security with the clergy and the people. Accordingly, The Bab was again removed from the prison of Chihrik and taken to Tabriz, the seat of the local government of the province. Here, on the 9th of July, 1850, He suffered martyrdom.

The Bab, with one of His most devoted followers, a youth of noble family, was conducted to an open square in the city and there the two were bound and suspended by ropes against a wall. A company of Armenian Christian soldiers was drawn up and the order to fire given. When the smoke cleared, however, to the astonishment of all present it was found that the aim had been too high, and instead of harming the captives the ropes had only been severed and the two captives had dropped to the ground unhurt. So great was the consternation caused by this incident that the commander of the executing company refused to take further part in the affair, and another company, of native soldiers, was ordered out and The Bab and His disciple were again suspended before the wall. The ensuing volleys riddled both bodies with bullets, and death was instantaneous. Later, the remains were cast out into a moat and there exposed to public view as a warning of the fate which awaited those who followed the new faith.

By night the body of The Bab was removed by some of the faithful, and after being swathed in silk it was disguised as a bale of merchandise and deposited in a place of safety. As conditions and wisdom demanded, from time to time this hiding place was changed, and finally, on the 21st of March, 1909, in the presence of a notable gathering of pilgrims from various parts of both the Orient and the Occident, the body of The Bab was laid to rest by Abdul-Baha, in a sarcophagus, in the crypt of the shrine of The Bab in the Holy Land.

Although The Bab was without learning and schooling, save that of a very elementary nature, yet He was so richly endowed with spiritual or inspirational wisdom that He discomfited the learned mullahs until they feared discussion with him, lest the people should see the weakness of their arguments and the strength of His teachings. He wrote with the greatest rapidity and fluency, dictating both in public and private His many treatises upon intricate theological questions.

During the four years of The Bab's imprisonment His numerous letters and epistles were, with the greatest difficulty, smuggled out of the prison and sent to the followers in various parts of the country. These writings contain His injunctions to the believers for their guidance and protection until the coming of "Him whom God shall manifest."

The Bab's ordinances were given for the people of his time only, and were commensurable with the needs and conditions of the believers during the interim between his manifestation and the manifestation of the greater One to come. The Bab was the "First Point" of this revelation, the precursor of the greater One. In his teachings He reiterated again and again that, when "He whom God shall manifest" appeared, all should turn unto Him, and that He would reveal teachings and ordinances which would replace the Babi sacred literature.

It is a matter of importance to note that *the one great event for which the Bäbi Movement paved the way, was the manifestation of Baha-'o'llah, treated of in the next chapter. It should not be considered as a later development of the*

Bábi cause, but rather the Bab's mission should be considered as simply introductory to it. Running through The Bab's writings are found countless allusions to the spiritual power, splendor and glory of Baha'o'llah, who was then in the world, but unknown to men. He was the inspiration of The Bab, to Whom The Bab continually testified in the most eloquent and stirring of his verses, and of Whom He bore witness by a life of suffering and imprisonment, crowned by martyrdom.

III.
BAHA 'O' LLAH

Mirza Hussein Ali of Noor, more widely known as Baha'o'llah, was born in Teheran, Persia, on the 12th of November, 1817. His family was one of wealth and note, His father as well as other relatives, having been ministers of the government, serving in various official capacities.

During Baha'o'llah's youth, His father died, leaving Him, the eldest son, as the head of the family. Being of a contemplative disposition, the public life which His father had led had no allurements for Baha'o'llah. He chose instead, one of comparative retirement, managing the family estates and affairs, and supervising the education of His brothers and sisters. Even in His youth the marks of wisdom and distinction were upon Him.

In His home Baha'o'llah was taught the Persian language, and wisdom, knowledge and the deepest of spiritual mysteries were His, through His own studies, meditations and inspirations. Later, these basic principles of being are revealed in His writings with power and force. These truths are the foundation of the Bahai cause. They are living, spiritual principles, for they appeal to and satisfy the soul, and meet all of the moral and spiritual needs of life.

Baha'o'llah never attended any school or institution of learning. His knowledge was inspirational. It came from the source of all knowledge, and is the source of knowledge for all.

At the time The Bab made His declaration and sent his disciples forth from Shiraz, Baha'o'llah, then about twenty-seven years of age, was residing in Teheran. When the glad tidings of

The Bab's manifestation reached the capital, Baha'o'llah was among the first to respond to the call, and He, in turn, proclaimed the cause, upholding it firmly. He visited the city of Noor, the home of His family, and other neighboring cities and towns, where He engaged in expounding The Bab's teachings, later returning to Teheran, there again to take up His work.

The Bab and Baha'o'llah had no family connection whatever, the former being of Arabic-Persian descent, while the latter was of ancient Persian lineage. *These two never met in person,* yet in spirit they were intimate even in Their deepest thoughts and inspirations. Between Them a correspondence was established which was carried on up to the last days of The Bab's mission here on earth.

When, during His imprisonment in Chih-rik, The Bab foresaw the approaching day of His removal to Tabriz and His martyrdom, He sent by faithful followers to Baha'o'llah a package containing a number of His writings, His pencase and seal ring. At that time, though Baha'o'llah was known only as His staunch supporter, yet The Bab saw in Him divine signs not yet manifest to others.

It was not long after The Bab's martyrdom that a great calamity befell the believers. A certain enthusiast, who (though a believer in The Bab) was quite ignorant of the teachings, became unbalanced through brooding over the persecution and slaughter of his brother believers, and in the hope of being able to better their condition made an attempt upon the life of the Shah of Persia. The guilty one was immediately killed by the royal attendants. Without inquiring further into the matter, his crime was taken, by the Shah and his ministers, as a demonstration of the Babis, as a body, against the government. Then the innocent were made to suffer for the guilty. This was the beginning of a season of the most bloody massacres and horrible torture of the believers. Even to be *suspected* of being a Babi was—in many cases—sufficient to cause the extinction of a whole family. In Teheran some eighty believers were handed over by the government to the Moslems to be killed, each being subjected to some unique torture before the final slaying.

It was a time of greatest trial and test for the Babis. Each calamity was followed by one, more terrible; yet through all, the wonderful hope of The Promised One to come and their enthusiastic love and devotion to the memory of their martyred master, The Bab, upheld and strengthened them to meet every kind of persecution.

In the midst of these troubles Baha'o'llah came boldly to the front. He was placed under arrest, and spent four months in chains in the dungeon of one of the Teheran prisons. Later on, it being proved that He was innocent of any plot against the government, He was sent by the royal order into exile to Baghdad in Asiatic Turkey. There it was thought He would be so far removed from the Babis in Persia as to destroy His prestige as leader among them. These events occurred in 1852, the ninth year after the declaration of The Bab.

Baha'o'llah's exile to Baghdad marks an important epoch in the development of the cause, for from that time He stands preeminent as a power in that persecuted community.

After the fury of the massacres of 1851-1852, the Babis were in a deplorable condition. Many of the disciples and personal associates of The Bab had been martyred, while, on account of the troubles, the few remaining ones who had personally been taught by Him were all but cut off from association with the younger followers. It had not been possible to disseminate, beyond a very limited circle, the writings of The Bab, so that the vast majority of the believers knew little of His real teachings. In addition, they were actuated by a powerful spirit of devotion to their cause; a devotion which, because of its very intensity, at times led them into difficulties. Here and there arose false claimants for The Bab's successorship, all of which led to confusion and trouble.

This was the condition that prevailed when Baha'o'llah reached Baghdad. Immediately He directed His attention and energy toward bringing knowledge and assurance to the followers. He taught them the real significance of The Bab's teachings and little by little, through understanding, their undirected enthusiasm found power in restraint and strength. Thus He prepared them to recognize by their spiritual faculties, The One whose coming The Bab had proclaimed.

The Babis now increased in firmness 'and steadfastness, especially those in Baghdad. As the fame of Baha'o'llah spread abroad, men of learning came to converse with Him and listen to His teachings, and of these many believed. As the believers increased in number, the anger of the Moslem clergy was aroused and this, in turn, gave rise to other serious difficulties. Baha'o'llah was then led to seek a solitary retreat in the mountain fastness of Kurdistan, where He remained for two years in spiritual preparation for His coming manifestation and ministry.

Upon Baha'o'llah's return to Baghdad, great was the joy of the Babis. By that time they were realizing their spiritual strength, and they welcomed their teacher with all the fervor and enthusiasm of Oriental devotees.

Believers from various parts of Arabia and Persia now came to Baha'o'llah, seeking knowledge from Him. Then they went forth again to teach with a deeper understanding than before, and with a renewed zeal and fervor; and the cause grew in strength.

These developments were closely watched by the Moslem priests. Fearful of the loss of their own hold upon the people, which they saw waning as the light of the new teachings spread, the priests incited the government against Baha'o'llah, with the determination to do all they could to curb His power. Accordingly, after some correspondence between the Persian and Turkish governments, an international arrangement was formulated, by which Baha'o'llah was ordered to proceed to Constantinople, there to await the pleasure of the Ottoman Sultan, to whom he became temporally subject.

Upon hearing that their chief was to be removed from Baghdad, the believers became wild with grief, the greatest consternation prevailing among them. A number of them prepared to accompany Him in His further exile. When, in obedience to the summons of the Sultan, Baha'o'llah left Baghdad previous to starting on His long journey, He encamped a short distance from the city in the Garden of El Rizwan. There He was surrounded by some of His most devoted followers—believers in The Bab.

To the *most trusted* of these followers Baha'o'llah, during His twelve days of sojourn in El Rizwan, revealed Himself and His mission: that He was The Promised One foretold by The Bab; that He was the One promised by all the prophets to appear in the latter days and establish GOD'S Kingdom, the great universal brotherhood of nations; that He was the One through whose inspired guidance the difficulties of the believers would be removed; by steadfastly and unitedly following Whose injunctions those blessings for which the believers had hoped, suffered and prayed would be realized. This hope He extended to the adherents, exhorting them to renew their energies, faith and assurance.

The Manifestation of Baha'o'llah took place in April, 1863, nineteen years after the declaration of The Bab.* This was the goal toward which all the Babis had directed their attention, beyond which no one had seen. Now, having attained to the meeting of The Promised One, the believers found themselves upon the threshold of an outlook so vast, and of a work so great, that it was only with the sustaining power of their new teacher that they were able to face the difficulties which confronted them.

The period of preparation over, the trusted believers found themselves in the full light of the day of GOD, compared with which the preparative light of The Bab had been but as a few rays.

Traveling overland by caravan, through Irak-Arabi and Asia Minor to Samsaon on the Black Sea, and from there by ship, Baha'o'llah and His band of followers, after a fatiguing journey, reached Constantinople.

Here the exiles remained for several months under governmental surveillance, before they were sent under military escort to Adrianople, in

---

*In the writings of The Bab are certain verses prophetic of the rise of Baha'o'llah in the ninth year of the Babi cause, and of His manifestation in the nineteenth year of the same. These prophecies were given symbolically, in such manner as to be understood only by the faithful.

the interior of Roumelia. There, it was thought, Baha'o'llah would be so far removed from the world which His cause was agitating as practically to destroy His power as a religious leader, thus striking a fatal blow at the new faith. It is to be noted that each attempt upon the part of the temporal powers to oppose this cause marks an epoch in the demonstration of its spiritual power.

Baha'o'llah and His exiled followers remained in Adrianople for five years, during which time the cause grew and the believers attained to moral and spiritual virtues, their faith manifesting itself in their daily lives. This was a time of growth and preparation. Through personal contact, those who were with Baha'ollah grew in the shadow of His wisdom, while those at a distance had their souls made strong and steadfast through His written teachings; for in Him all found the realization of the spiritual power, glory and majesty of "Him whom God shall manifest".

While in Adrianople Baha'o'llah directed His power to bringing the believers to a realization of His mission. The cause under The Bab's inspiration was more or less local, being confined to a few Islamic countries. Its character and institutions were commensurable with the conditions to which it ministered. It fulfilled its purpose and when this was accomplished in the appearance of Baha'o'llah, the Babi Movement, as such, ceased to exist.

With the manifestation of Baha'o'llah, not only did the followers cease to be known as Babis, becoming *Bahais* in name, but in the deepest spiritual sense did they receive from Baha'o'llah that soul-quickening touch, which created within them the power to go forth to all the world, carrying the message of peace, attracting people of all nations and religions, and fulfilling that which He sent them forth to accomplish.

Dating from the time of the declaration of Baha'o'llah in the Garden of El Rizwan, the cause assumes a universal or a world character; for it must be understood that the teachings of Baha'o'llah are not limited to the needs of certain conditions and countries, nor to the oriental peoples. He comes, The One promised by all religions, for all peoples under all conditions, both oriental and occidental. His teaching is universal; it is for the whole world.

Baha'o'llah achieved His work only under the greatest difficulties. Among those followers who accompanied Baha'o'llah in exile was His half-brother, who failed to comprehend Him and the scope and magnitude of His mission. This man resented Baha'o'llah's growing power, and his opposition, together with the spread of the faith, created troubles with the Turkish government, which increased until an order was issued separating him from the believers, and sending Baha'o'llah a prisoner, to the fortress of Akka on the coast of Syria.

It was in the summer of 1868 that Baha'o'llah and about seventy of His followers, men, women and children, were taken in captivity; overland to Gallipoli, where they were embarked in a ship sailing for Egypt. Arriving in the harbor of Alexandria, the exiles were transferred to another vessel which landed them in Haifa, but a few miles across the bay from Akka, a distance which was covered in small boats.

Akka is the *Acre* of the time of the crusaders, more anciently known as Ptolemais. Her antiquated ramparts and crumbling fortifications, the scenes of some of the bloodiest combats of military history from the ancient times of the Phœnicians down to the Napoleonic war in Syria, testify to an earthly power which is of the past; while her name, so intimately connected with the Bahai cause, to-day is most closely associated with that great constructive movement for spiritual power and peace, the glad tidings of which were first sent forth to all the world from behind her prison gates.

For some years prior to Baha'o'llah's arrival, the fortress of Akka had been used as a prison and a place of exile to which the Sultan of Turkey sent his political opponents. The deadly climate of that fever-stricken rock slowly but surely accomplished the desired destruction of many of these unfortunate ones.

Here Baha'o'llah and His people were thrust into two rooms of the barrack prison. With poor and insufficient food, and water not fit to drink, fever and sickness broke out among the believers. Their sufferings were most intense, yet through all they were spiritually in the greatest joy and peace, for they realized that only by meeting the very worst of this world's conditions, could Baha'o'llah relieve and change those conditions; while, as for themselves, they were only too happy and contented to share His sufferings.

It was during this close confinement of Baha'o'llah within the prison of Akka that He made His declaration to the world. This was done by sending a series of epistles, written in Adrianople, to the rulers and potentates of the earth. In these missives He clearly states His mission, and He announces to all this latter-day call of The LORD—the call of unity, harmony, and peace.

Very soon the officials and officers of the city began to realize the greatness of Baha'o'llah. and some among them believed in Him. His fame as a teacher spread, and actuated by that veneration for wisdom, so peculiar to the Orient, many sought His presence, to be awakened to those truths the existence of which they previously had not realized.

After two years of close confinement in prison, Baha'o'llah was given the liberty of the city and allowed to live in a house provided for Him and His family. His followers entered into various occupations in the town and vicinity, and the material condition of the community was greatly improved.

In the early days of the imprisonment of Baha'o'llah in Akka, when He was most closely guarded and with the greatest difficulty His communications were transmitted to those outside the prison, His followers often journeyed from Persia overland, for months, to obtain but a glimpse of Him standing at His barred window or to gaze at Him from afar as He walked upon the parapet of the prison, and then they returned to their homes with renewed fervor and zeal in promulgating His cause. Later, these pilgrims from various countries had access to Him, and, quickened by His power, went forth to proclaim His Cause in the uttermost parts of the earth.

Besides those who saw Him personally, Baha'o'llah reached thousands in distant lands, and satisfied their thirst for knowledge, through His *tablets,* which were epistles of exhortation, advice and explanation written in response to letters from believers and seekers.

Baha'o'llah wrote also general treatises relating to matters both religious and secular. In these inspired writings are found the basic principles upon which are built the institutions of the Bahai faith.

During the latter years of His ministry, Baha-

'o'llah was allowed to spend much time in the country in the vicinity of Akka, even visiting Haifa and Mt. Carmel. At the villa of Behje (situated on the plain of Akka) He departed this life in the month of May, 1892, after forty years of hardship, imprisonment, and exile, that the soul of the world might be quickened with the life of the spirit. The tomb of Baha'o'llah, at Behjé, is greatly venerated by the many pilgrims who yearly visit it from all parts of the world.

Through Baha'o'llah this great teaching was given to man. His function was that of *the revealer*. Though as a man He lived a life in harmony with the conventions of His oriental environment, yet as The Revelator, the mouthpiece of The Spirit, His teachings are universally applicable to all peoples under all conditions. With the close of His ministry the *latter-day revelation* was complete *as a revelation*. The next step in the development of the cause was that of *explaining, establishing* and *demonstrating* these *revealed truths* in the world of practicality. For the accomplishment of this, Abdul-Baha, the son of Baha'o'llah, was the chosen instrument.

IV.
ABDUL-BAHA.

Abdul-Baha Abbas, also known as Abbas Effendi, the eldest son of Baha'o'llah, was born in Teheran, Persia, on the 23d day of May, 1844, the very day upon which The Bab made His declaration to the disciples in Shiraz.

At a very early age Abdul-Baha was called upon to share the sufferings of his father. When Baha'o'llah's persecution began with His imprisonment in Teheran and exile to Baghdad, His property was confiscated, even to personal effects, while the members of His family suffered intensely for the bare necessities of life.

Abdul-Baha's schooling was interrupted in his childhood by these persecutions, and afterward he never attended any school. However, through the constant companionship of his father, from whom his inspiration came, and from his loving service to all people both high and low, an understanding, wisdom and knowledge are his which are of God.

Abdul-Baha accompanied Baha'o'llah upon His winter journey from Teheran to Baghdad, and during the years of exile there was constantly at his father's right hand, serving and helping Him in His work of teaching the people.

Abdul-Baha was the first to recognize the divine power of Baha'o'llah. He was the first soul quickened by the spirit of Baha'o'llah, and the first to arise in the service of the Kingdom. In Abdul-Baha's life of devotion to the cause and his practice of the precepts of Baha'o'llah, the perfect life of The Spirit is manifest, and in him all things are found to be accomplished.

In Adrianople Abdul-Baha took upon himself the task of relieving Baha'o'llah of all possible cares of daily life, so that He might devote Himself entirely to His mission. During the imprisonment in Akka, when hardship and sickness were encompassing the believers on every side, it was Abdul-Baha, who, through his buoyancy of spirit, gave courage to the distressed ones. It was he who nursed the sick and through the touch of his hand imparted strength to the weak, while the light of his great love illumined all and empowered them to overcome their ills.

In the written testament of Baha'o'llah, as well as in His verbal teachings, which have come down to us through those who were near to Him, He appointed His son Abdul-Baha to succeed Him in His spiritual mission, and designated Him as the one who should complete His work in the world. The father's mantle has fallen upon the shoulders of the son. The staff of Baha'o'llah is now in the hands of Abdul-Baha, and the Spirit of God, which spoke through Baha'o'llah revealing TRUTH to the world, is now manifesting to the world through Abdul-Baha's life of service to God and to man.

Abdul-Baha is the center of the Bahai cause. He is the one to be emulated. Through following him the Believers will attain to the spiritual fullness of the Bahai life. Abdul-Baha is the beloved son into whose hands has been intrusted the guidance of the people of The Kingdom.

Abdul-Baha's mission is that of the explainer, the establisher. Through his life of service he is teaching and leading the people to the realization of the revelation of Baha'o'llah. By his life of example he is teaching the heart of mankind and infusing spiritual consciousness into humanity.

Abdul-Baha comes with the power of God to live and manifest the life of The Kingdom. This he is demonstrating to the world, for through his ministry all things as revealed and intended by Baha'o'llah are being accomplished.

Almost his entire life Abdul-Baha has passed under the temporal law as an exile and a religious prisoner. At times he was only under military surveillance, and again imprisoned behind barred doors. Yet despite these physical hindrances his spiritual work has prospered and his message of glad tidings has gone the world round, taking with it the peace of the Spirit to thousands of souls of every race and religion.

That Abdul-Baha's mission is a purely spiritual one needs no further demonstration than that which is already visible in the world. With all of the worldly powers against him, but with the power of God with him, he is accomplishing that which he was sent to accomplish, for from him is emanating that power which is uniting men's hearts and drawing into The Kingdom the hungering souls from all peoples. Abdul-Baha is harmonizing Christians, Jews, Moslems, Zoroastrians, Buddhists and Hindus in the one and the true faith, the Fatherhood of God and the Brotherhood of man. The results of his work prove his cause.

The name Abdul-Baha signifies the title of its bearer, "The Servant of God". Abdul-Baha makes but one claim for himself, that of absolute servitude in the path of God. The Spirit of Baha'o'llah is the source of Abdul-Baha's inspiration and his strength. He seeks no prestige nor prominence for himself. His demonstration to the world is through deeds. His method of teaching is through deeds. His mission is to establish the deeds of The Kingdom in the lives of his followers.

With the passing of Baha'o'llah (May, 1892) began Abdul-Baha's divine mission as "The Center of the Covenant". When he arose invested with the power of the Spirit, began the third and final period of the establishment of The Kingdom here among men.

Abdul-Baha is an exile from his country and, until the re-establishment of the Turkish Constitution in the summer of 1908, he was a religious prisoner, held in the fortress of Akka. With this political change, he—with many other prisoners and exiles—was freed and is no longer under military surveillance.

Since his release Abdul-Baha has made but few changes in his daily life. Now it is possible for many more of his followers to visit him than formerly, consequently his duties and labors are increased. He has given up his residence in Akka and, after residing for some months in the neighboring town of Haifa, he has gone to Egypt, from whence he is at present carrying on his work.*

During every phase of the progress of The Cause, Abdul-Baha has done nothing needlessly to agitate the fanatical peoples who surround him. In every way he and his family observe the oriental conventions of life, in order to maintain harmony and amicable relations with the surrounding people. He is changing the world by infusing spiritual wisdom into men's souls. He teaches and reaches the people through leading them rather than by trying to force them, through winning souls by the spirit

---

*Since the first edition of this book was published, Abdul-Baha has visited America where he travelled and taught extensively. At the present time (March, 1913) he is on a similar mission in Europe.

rather than by trying to bring to bear the more objective forces of the outer world.

As there were a few of The Bab's professed followers, who failed in the days of Baha-'o'llah to recognize in Him the divine power by virtue of which He was The Bab's successor, so there are also a few followers of Baha'o'llah, whose eyes have not been opened during the ministry of Abdul-Baha to the spirit manifesting within him, and who have failed to see in him the successor of Baha'o'llah.

These opposing people have at times made much trouble for Abdul-Baha. During the years of his imprisonment, through false reports concerning his work, made to the government by these people (led by his own half-brother), the Turkish officials imagined the Bahais were plotting against the Ottoman power. Thus, much distress was created.

Sometimes, on account of the troubles brought on by the opposing people, it has been impossible for the believers to visit Abdul-Baha. Once, some of his followers were cast into prison, and at another time some of the believers were forced to flee from the Holy Land and seek refuge in Egypt. Nevertheless, through all trials and troubles Abdul-Baha has gone steadily forward accomplishing his work, the number of his opposers decreasing and the number of his sympathizers increasing, until now he has clearly shown to all that *his cause is not dependent upon earthly prosperity for its growth,* nor does opposition hinder its spread.

The Bahais have the uttermost esteem, love and veneration for Abdul-Baha. To them he is friend, counselor, and spiritual guide.

In looking toward him as the expounder of divine wisdom his followers are worshipping the

Divine Light which is manifesting through his life of service to God and man. They are not deifying his human personality, for that he holds in common with all men.

Abdul-Baha does not wish to call the attention of people to his personality, nor to himself as a man, save to demonstrate to them the principles of the higher life for which he stands. He not only does not seek personal prestige, but even anything suggestive of this is extremely odious to him. For example, he has repeatedly requested the believers not to use in connection with his name the terms "Lord" or "Master", which are so often applied in the Orient to spiritual teachers. In fact, any demonstration of personal adoration is offensive to him.

Abdul-Baha stands as the exponent of a spiritual principle, a great divine power. This, and this only, he desires the world to recognize.

Many beautiful and touching incidents are related by the people of Akka of the way in which, through long-suffering and kindness, Abdul-Baha has won the hearts of those who, because of their prejudice, formerly were his enemies. Caring for the sick and protecting the oppressed form a large part of his daily duties. One of the titles applied to him by the indigent Arabs is "Father of the Poor".

While Abdul-Baha's method of teaching and moving people is through the heart and is gentleness itself, nevertheless, conditions often make it necessary for him to be stern. Some of the native Arabs, and others with whom he has relations need to be dealt with by a loving but firm hand.

Abdul-Baha administers justice, but with such kindness that the individual realizes it is done in the true spirit of paternal training; and instead of offending the guilty one the opposite effect is produced, and a lasting good accomplished.

Abdul-Baha is married. He has four daughters, three of whom have husbands and families. Abdul-Baha is teaching through his home life as a devoted husband and a loving father, a lesson to both the people of the East and of the West. He is teaching the Oriental, monogamy and that woman should be man's intellectual, moral and spiritual companion as well as the mother of his children; and he is teaching the Occidental, in these days of marital unrest, that marriage should be founded upon a spiritual basis and not alone upon a physical one.

While imprisoned Abdul-Baha received a stipend from the Turkish government. Now that he is freed, this no longer continues. He holds cultivated lands in the vicinity of Akka which render him an income. His personal needs and those of his family are few. In reality, that which he possesses is for the benefit of all, while he is but the guardian of it. No one knows of the many children he is educating; how many needy and infirm ones he is clothing, housing and feeding. Abdul-Baha is demonstrating to the world that there is neither virtue nor disgrace in either riches or poverty; and that man, either in need or in plenty, should utilize his little or his much glorifying God through serving humanity.

There are many expenses in connection with the carrying on of the work. Those whose souls are in the cause contribute in various ways, of which few, if any, are known. The American Bahais can testify that Abdul-Baha very rarely permits any of them to share in carrying the burden of the work in the East, though in rare instances he has accepted contributions for this purpose.

While his personality Abdul-Baha wishes

sacrificed, for the cause for which he stands, nevertheless the people look at the outer person, and each returning pilgrim from Akka is asked many questions regarding Abdul-Baha, the man.

Abdul-Baha expresses perfect manhood. The vigor of a fully-developed physical, intellectual, and spiritual power is apparent in his every movement; yet with this is a delicacy, a sensibility and an intuition which denote the inspiration that dominates him. In him is all of the dignity and majesty of the king combined with the humbleness of the servant, and upon his brow is the strength and force of the ancient Mosaic type of man, counterbalanced by the gentleness of a child.

In Abdul-Baha's presence one becomes conscious of the deepest feeling of respect, veneration and even awe, yet not the awe which holds one at a distance, for within Abdul-Baha's soul there burns such a fire of divine love that very few escape its power of attraction.

The awakened soul realizes that Abdul-Baha understands the spiritual condition of men, and that he is the divine physician who, through the love of God, is healing the souls of men of the disease of ignorance and superstition and inharmony. He ministers to each in accordance with the needs of the individual. Often, at the time, one does not understand why Abdul-Baha acts and advises as he does, but later all becomes clear when, through carrying out his instructions, one sees the depth of his understanding and realizes the profoundness of his wisdom.

Abdul-Baha seeks always to remove the cause of trouble. His vision penetrates into the soul and understands its condition. His balm is summed up in the word LOVE. Divine love annihilates worry and kills fear, and when it takes possession of the soul it is as though another and a new dimension were added to the individual, and old conditions of doubt and uncertainty are replaced by poise and assurance. Abdul-Baha's mission is to teach men to bring the love of The Kingdom into everyday life, and to manifest it in every thought, word and deed.

It is in the little things and the numerous details of life that the test comes in applying spiritual teachings. In the life of Abdul-Baha it is through the seemingly small things that his great spirit manifests itself, and goes out with a penetrating power to the souls of those who allow themselves to come within the radius of its activity. In his presence it is as if a refreshing breeze, a spiritual force, proceeded from the heart of Abdul-Baha to that of the seeker—an indescribable force carrying strength to the weak and guidance to the strong.

Abdul-Baha's every word, look and gesture bespeaks his spirit, and while his spirit is the most elusive and difficult of all things to express in words, when once perceived it is the most tangible of realities, for it is the very essence of the life of the soul which is proceeding from him who is the center of guidance.

Often the face of Abdul-Baha in repose, bears an expression as if caused by a great weight of sorrow impossible to describe. No soul can fathom the depths into which he sees, nor the profoundness of his realization of the suffering condition of man. He feels the hungering and the thirsting of the soul of humanity for spiritual rest, and upon his brow is written her silent agony. However, when Abdul-Baha speaks he is fairly charged with the positive life-forces of The Kingdom. In every glance and movement he manifests the joy of the Lord, and as he shows forth this love and joy in his many deeds of kindness, his spirit penetrates the hearts of those who come in contact with him, and they in turn go forth filled with the spirit to work and to serve in his path.

The pilgrim discovers in Abdul-Baha one who impresses his hearers not by projecting his own ideas or personality upon them, but by calling forth a response from within the soul of each individual seeker. The direct influence of the will of one personality upon another is transitory and without lasting benefit. But how different is the message of the spirit speaking through the life and the words of Abdul-Baha, who has sacrificed his will to the will of God. He has a message for every soul, and as the seeker meets spiritually with the soul of Abdul-Baha, a new force is added to his nature and he goes forth quickened, alive and aflame with the love of God.

Through The Bab the way was made ready and prepared for the coming of the Lord, the Latter-Day Messiah, Baha'o'llah. Through Baha'o'llah, in whom God was Manifest, divine knowledge was revealed to man, the laws of The Kingdom given to the world, and Abdul-Baha was appointed, "The Center of the Covenant". Now through Abdul-Baha's life of service to God and man, the way is made plain for all and the Kingdom of God established upon earth.

V.
THE MANIFESTATION OF THE WORD OF GOD.

"That which is the cause of everlasting life, eternal honor, universal enlightenment, real salvation and prosperity, is first of all, the knowledge of God." *Abdul-Baha.*

"The root of all knowledge is the knowledge of God: Glory be to Him! And this knowledge is impossible save through *His Manifestation.*" *Baha'o'llah.*

It is written: "In the beginning was The Word, and The Word was with God, and The Word was God." It is through the Word of God manifested in the temple of man, that men's souls become quickened with the spiritual life, attain divine knowledge, receive spiritual assurance, and are enabled to rise above the condition of ignorance and ascend the scale of advancement and civilization. The Word, or the Spirit of God, spoke through all the prophets or manifestations.

Infinite Deity is beyond the comprehension of man: *yet, through the manifestation* of The Spirit of The Deity, man is enabled to come into touch with God, to comprehend and to know His characteristics and His attributes, and to obtain Divine Knowledge which is eternal life. By this is not meant that the essence of the Infinite Deity is contained nor confined in the personality of the revelator, but that the soul of the prophet is as a clear mirror which mirrors forth, or manifests, all of the divine attributes. Everywhere in the world of nature is seen the result of God's creative power, yet this has never awakened nor brought spiritual quickening, divine joy, nor comfort to the soul of man. This is because God's creation, though it emanates from Him, yet it does not *manifest Him*. The heart of man is only divinely quickened, and spiritually satisfied, through the coming to humanity of the *Manifestation of God* or The Word Revealed.

The Manifestation of "The Word" or of "The Spirit," through the prophets or "Chosen Ones," is the unique source of the spiritual enlightenment of men. This source is of God, not of man. Though the prophets and divine teachers were men, their spiritual power and strength was not because of any human virtue or wisdom. Their power to change men's natures, and to create great spiritual awakenings in the world was due to the Spirit of God which spoke through them. The Word of God is a life-giving, a creative power. Through it, slumbering humanity is quickened with spiritual wisdom, and the souls of men are lifted from the condition of ignorance to that of knowledge and wisdom. The advancement of the world of humanity is due to the quickening power of The Word. From it proceeds the very seed of civilization and progress and through it man is divinely quickened and born into The Kingdom of God.

The great power of the world's divine teachers has been due to their divine wisdom and inspiration. These Manifestations have each arisen as teachers among men. As they found sympathetic souls prepared for the spiritual messages which they brought, they revealed truths, always giving in proportion to the capacity of their disciples to receive.

In the ministry of each prophet is seen a certain development, and unfoldment of his teaching. This is due to the spiritual unfoldment and development of the souls of his followers, for speaking through each prophet was the *Perfect Eternal Word,* which in itself is above unfoldment and development. Men can comprehend this only as their souls develop. Therefore each prophet revealed himself little by little, as he prepared his followers to receive him in the fullness of his mission.

The inner spiritual teachings of the Divine Manifestations have been one and the same in substance, differing only in degree. The degree of the spiritual knowledge manifested has been always commensurate with the degree of the spiritual capacity of the people to whom the prophet ministered. The outer teachings, including the divine laws and ordinances of the divine revelators, have differed in every age. These specific instructions have always been given in conformity with the material condition peculiar to the various ages.

Through the harmony of the spiritual law and the material law, as exemplified in the lives and teachings of the Manifestations, humanity has come under divine guidance, the direct result of which has been a higher state of development of morals and all social relations.

Thus, from the purely spiritual view-point the Bahais regard all the prophets as the same, because of the one eternal, unchangeable truth which they, one and all, manifested; whereas, viewed from the human standpoint, these spiritual teachers are seen to be different personalties, giving different teachings and establishing different religious systems.

The laws and ordinances, as given to the world by the prophets, though material have had a deep spiritual effect upon man. They were given through divine wisdom; and by obedience to them, *the living out of the same* by men, the conditions were created which were necessary for the fuller and unhampered spiritual unfoldment of humanity. It is for this reason that each revelator has insisted that the people follow his commands. It was for their own good that he commanded this. Their welfare depended upon following his injunctions.

Supply and demand go hand in hand in spiritual matters, as science has proven them to do on the material plane. At the time of the coming of each divine manifestation there was a certain spiritual need among men. With each "Coming", the ministering to that need was the unique mission of the prophet.

The difference in the missions or the fields of work of the prophets, naturally differentiates them into the *world* manifestations, those whose teachings and ordinances were directly applied to the whole world, such as the Melchizadek type, Christ and Baha'o'llah, and the more *local* manifestations, those whose teachings and laws were applicable only to certain people under certain conditions, such as Zoroaster, Moses, Mohammed and others. Some prophets founded new religious systems which previously had not existed, while there were others who re-established and confirmed the faith of the people in the teachings and institutions of a former prophet. Of these latter the Hebrew prophets after Moses are examples.

As there are cycles of growth, fruition and decay in life on the physical plane, there are also the cycles of birth, development, fruition, decay in religious systems or dispensations.

As the cycles or seasons in the physical world are due to the condition of the material earth, so the cycles or seasons in the religious world are due to the condition of the world of humanity.

Every religion has had its birth in the advent of its divine founder. Through the labors of its early adherents it grew and developed, bringing forth its fruits in the institutions and civilization which grew up and formed about it. This was its golden age. Then followed a period in which the faith of the people grew cold, spirituality waned, morals suffered, and religion losing its spirit became a form. Thus the souls of the people became starved and their condition needed the ministration of another prophet, who in due time appeared and lifted them a step higher and nearer toward the coming of The Kingdom upon earth.

In this way each prophet has been a link in the *great chain of revelators,* completing the work and fulfilling the words of his predecessors and preparing the way for others to come after him. Thus have all manifestations of the past prepared the way for the *latter-day coming* of The Lord, accomplished in the coming of Baha'o'llah, whose mission was *to unite those now following many systems,* into *one brotherhood* and *one universal faith.*

The prophets have been seers as well as sources of divine life. Through spiritual understanding they were able to indicate in their teachings the material signs and conditions as well as the more spiritual ones, which would characterize the advent of succeeding manifestations.

The "return" of the prophets does not refer to the return to this world of a "personality". It refers to the return *in another personality,* of the impersonal Spirit, the Word or Spirit of God which spoke through the prophets of the past. With the passing of centuries people ceased to differentiate between the personality of a manifestation and the Spirit of God which spoke through him, hence, instead of looking for the return of The Spirit manifesting through *another* personality, in these latter days the people of each religion are mistakenly looking for the personal, individual return of their own special prophet.

The mission of each divine revelator has been to announce and to prepare the way for the brotherhood of The Kingdom among men. Each accomplished his mission, speaking and teaching through symbols and parables commensurable with the conditions of his day; each quickened the souls of the people with divine life and each foretold the coming of the great Latter-Day Messiah who was to establish The Kingdom of Peace upon earth.

In the coming of The Bab, Baha'o'llah and Abdul-Baha is found the fulfillment of the divine promises of God, given to the peoples of the past ages, and in it is the beginning of that age of divine enlightenment and spiritual wisdom for which men have long hoped and prayed. In the light of their inspired teachings all religious teachings of the past are understood and seen to be as parts of one great divine plan for the spiritual enlightenment of the world, and in the Bahai revelation is realized, also, that power which is binding and uniting the peoples of all races and religions in one universal religion, which is The Kingdom of God upon earth.

Resurrection and judgment pertain to the coming of a manifestation. These terms should be understood spiritually. Through *the Word* revealed, souls are quickened and the spiritually dead are given divine life. The day of each prophet is the time of judgment for those souls who hear his message, whether they accept the truth or reject it.

To-day is the time of judgment prophesied in all of the holy books of all peoples. The call of The Lord has gone forth. The people are hearing it. Some are awake to it and are arising to serve, while other souls are not yet sufficiently aroused to realize what has come into the world.

That *The Word of God has again been manifested to man* and that *"The One" promised* in the holy writings of all religions *has come in the flesh* and has established the new and the divine order of things, *The Kingdom of God on earth,* is the message which the Bahais are giving to the world.

VI.
RELATION OF THE BAHAI MOVEMENT TO THE RELIGIONS OF THE PAST

The people of each religion expect the return of the *Spirit* which shone through their prophet in the past, and the universal establishment of their own religion. The Word of God speaking through all the prophets gave the same message of the coming of the Messiah and the establishment of The Kingdom upon earth.

As time passed, and the spirit of the teachings became weak, the people ceased to regard their prophet as a human being, the medium through whom the *Spirit* of God manifested and was revealed. They began to deify the human personality of the prophet and instead of expecting the return of the same *Spirit,* manifesting through *another personality,* they began to look for the return in person of their guide or prophet. Thus the Christians believe in the corporeal descent of Jesus from the heavens (interstellar space), instead of the appearance of the Christ *Spirit,* which was the divine power in Jesus that He promised would again manifest upon earth at the end of His dispensation. In the same way the Jews look for the personal return of Elijah "before the coming of the great and dreadful day of the Lord," and the Moslems look for the personal and corporeal return of the Imam Mahdi.

As the Bahai message is being given to the people of each of these religions, they are being called back to the original teachings of their individual prophet. They realize that the voice of the *Spirit* spoke through Him, and they understand all the prophets to be manifestations of the *one Spirit* of God to the people of their times, and in this day they see the manifestations again of this same Divine Spirit through the founders of the Bahai movement, by which are realized all the promises and prophecies of all the religions regarding the Latter-Day "Coming," and The Kingdom upon earth.

CHRISTIANITY AND THE BAHAI MOVEMENT.

The Bahais believe that in Jesus appeared "The Word," or The Spirit of God. This differentiated Him from other men. By virtue of the Divine Spirit which spoke through Him, he was *The Christ*, the manifestation of God among men. Through Him souls became spiritually quickened, were reborn, and were lifted from the condition of spiritual ignorance (sometimes called sin), into one of spiritual enlightenment (sometimes called salvation).

Like the mission of every prophet, that of Jesus The Christ was a three-fold one. First, He fulfilled the prophecies of the prophets who preceded Him and proclaimed His coming. Thus, in Him was the consummation of the former dispensations. Second, He was the unique source of divine enlightenment to the people of His dispensation, and through the power of His word he founded His cause. Third, He prepared the way for the coming of the great Latter-Day Messiah, Bah'o'llah, God manifesting Himself as The Father, whom He and all prophets foretold would arise in the fullness of time and establish The Kingdom of God upon earth.

Jesus explains the divine plan for the spiritualization of the world in its entirety in the parable of the "householder which planted a vineyard" (St. Matt. XXI, 33-41), in which the householder is symbolic of God, the creator of the world. The "vineyard" symbolizes the people of the world, while the "husbandmen" are the leaders of the people. His "servants" represent the prophets sent by the Lord to call the world to righteousness and divine obedience, all of whom the people persecuted and rejected. His "son" is Jesus, The Christ, whose teaching was refused by the world which crucified Him. *"When the Lord therefore of the vineyard cometh"* refers to the coming of the Latter-Day Messiah, Baha'o'llah, while "he will miserably destroy those wicked men and will let out his vineyard unto other husbandmen, which shall render him the fruits in their seasons," is prophetic of the great outpouring of divine grace through this new revelation, which will be so great as to overcome and dispel the great power of evil (spiritual ignorance) which is dominating humanity. This day is the time of the world's turning from humanity to divinity. Baha'o'llah has brought to the world a New Day, for with His coming, old conditions passed away and a new dispensation was ushered into existence. The law of equity, "an eye for an eye and a tooth for a tooth," and the Christ law of mercy and love have for centuries been known to man, but the power to enable the world in general to live according to the Christ law has been given to all humanity only through Baha'o'llah.

When God came to the world manifesting Himself as the "Son," Jesus Christ, the world rejected Him, "but as many as received Him, to them gave He power to become the sons of God, even to them that believe on His name." To those *individual souls He gave His peace,* but not to *the world,* because the world did not receive Him. This He announced when He said: "Think not that I am come to send peace on earth; I came *not to send peace,* but *a sword."* Here again, as well as in other instances, Christ states that His dispensation was to be a militant one, which would in the end of the age be followed by another, a triumphant dispensation of divine grace and *peace* here on earth. Now Baha'o'llah has brought that peace to the world. He is *"The Prince of Peace,"* who has come to the world and has established the foundation of *peace on earth.* How clearly Isaiah, the prophet, saw this coming of the Lord when He wrote, "For unto us a child is born, unto us a son is given, and the government shall be upon His shoulder and His name shall be called Wonderful, Counsellor, The Mighty God, the Everlasting Father, The Prince of Peace."

No one touched by the spirit of Christianity can fail to recognize that the Bahai teaching is only the *perfection of Christianity,* for to be a real Christian in spirit is to be a Bahai, and to be a real Bahai is to be a Christian. As one reads the words of Christ and the testimony of the apostles, who received from him many teachings, there stands out one promise above all other things—*his second coming among men—another appearance* of the *Christ spirit. The Word of God in the temple of man.* This manifestation to be the beginning of the end of the old order of human differences and at the same time to usher in the new order of divine peace here on earth. All is summed up in the promise "The Kingdoms of this world are become the Kingdoms of Our Lord, and of His Christ and He shall reign forever and ever."

JUDAISM AND THE BAHAI MOVEMENT.

The Bahais regard the Hebrew prophets as revealers of divine truth. Through these various channels The Word was revealed, souls were quickened with divine life and obeyed the divine laws, and the way was prepared for the coming of The Kingdom on earth. These prophets from the earliest, Abraham, down to the last, Malachi, formed a complete chain. Each built upon the foundation of the teachings of His predecessors; each ministered to the spiritual needs of the people of his day, and each extended to humanity the promise of the coming of the Messiah, at the end of the days, and of the righting of all things in the establishment of the reign of God among men.

As one reads the Hebrew Scriptures, the prophecies of the coming Messianic Dispensation are found to be the one great thread running through all. In this promise is heard the one divine voice of The Word of God speaking through the personalities of the many prophets or mouthpieces, or channels of truth.

In the Jewish holy books are found prophecies *pertaining in particular* to *two manifestations* of *"The Word,"* to come. The so-called *first* and *second comings of the Messiah;* those relating to the first coming were fulfilled in the coming and mission of Jesus, The Christ, while those regarding the second coming are fulfilled in these latter days in the coming of "The Ancient of Days", Baha'o'llah with His precursor, The Bab, in whom was The Spirit of Elijah (Malachi IV:5), and His "Servant, The Branch", (Zech. III:8), who is Abdul-Baha.

It was through the study of the prophecies regarding the second coming, as recorded by the prophet Daniel, that the Millerites learned that the Messiah was to come in the year 1844. They expected His miraculous appearance in the clouds and were disappointed. The Bab came and Abdul-Baha was born at this appointed time, fulfilling prophecy, but in a manner not anticipated by men. The country of Carmel and Sharon in the Holy Land, to which Baha'o'llah was sent in exile, and where He lived and taught, was the place designated by the ancient seers of Biblical fame, where the *"Ancient of Days" would appear.* The glory of the Lord of Hosts to come, and the power and majesty of His spiritual rule upon earth are testified to by prophet and psalmist in the most inspiring passages of Hebrew sacred writ, while the peace, prosperity and general upliftment of humanity resulting therefrom are most vividly depicted.

The mission of the Jewish people was a religious one. From the seed of the progenitor of this people have come the founders of great religions of the past, as well as the founders of the great religion of the present and future. From Abraham, through the line of Isaac came Moses and Jesus; through Ishmael came Mohammed and The Bab; while from the line of another son (Abraham had six sons other than Isaac and Ishmael) was descended Jesse,* from whom descended Baha'o'llah.

ISLAM AND THE BAHAI MOVEMENT.

The prophet Mohammed taught submission to the will of God. Islam means "Submission". Mohammed arose in Arabia at a time of spiritual need when the people were sunken in ignorance and superstition. Through his guidance, idolatry and immorality were changed into the worship of the one God, and into high moral standards. He brought a code of laws and ordinances

---
*Not Jesse, the father of David, but another of the same name. This point was explained to the writer by Abdul-Baha at Haifa. May, 1910.

perfectly adapted to the spiritual and material needs of the people of His day. These people, because of their extreme degradation, had been untouched both by Judaism and Christianity. They needed a teaching and a code of laws suited to their own special condition.

The rise of the Moslem civilization has had no parallel in history. United under the standard of the belief in one God and the immortality of the soul, the fierce sons of the Arabian desert, in an incredibly short time, evolved into a highly cultured people, their sciences, arts and literature having contributed much toward our present western civilization.

As division, superstition and decay crept into the Moslem Church the people retrograded, until in a few centuries after the death of Mohammed the spirit of his teaching was a thing of the past, and Moslem civilization was in a decline.

Islam, like Christianity and every other religion, can not be judged by its later followers. The student must go to its source in order to ascertain its truths. In Christianity, the history of the divisions and wars between the churches is one thing, and the teaching of Christ is another thing. So it is in Islam. The present condition of its people, and the condition to which the prophet called them are indeed very different. The Moslems look for three manifestations in the latter days (it being literally expressed in their teachings as three trumpet calls). According to the traditions of Islam, *seven* years and *forty* years, respectively, were to separate these calls or comings. This corresponds to the missions of The Bab and of Baha'o'llah which lasted seven, and forty years.

Islam teaches of a day (a time or period) of spiritual resurrection and judgment, and of the coming of the Christ, preceded by the Mahdi (director or guide), and of the establishment of The Kingdom upon earth.

The Moslem believes *the latter-day time* of spiritual awakening or resurrection, through the giving forth of the Word of God, to be the time of the world's judgment, the people being their own judges, as they choose to accept or to reject the newly revealed truth. This time was to be accompanied by certain signs similar to those mentioned in the Bible, such as: The coming of the spirit of Anti-Christ (which is infidelity), decay of religious faith among men, and the accompanying demoralization which this must bring with it.

Many Moslems have come into the Bahai faith, accepting The Bab as the promised Mahdi and Baha'o'llah as the Christ (Spirit), who was to come, for both have fulfilled their prophecies and traditions of which there are many. According to them, The Bab appeared from the East and made his public declaration at Mecca, at the place and time prophesied (1844 A. D. or 1260 A. H.), and taught during the anticipated length of time. Also, Baha'o'llah arose in Irak and went to Akka and Carmel in Syria. His mission lasted 40 years. The many details are so clearly traced in tradition and prophecy, that it is very easy for the orthodox Moslem to realize the truth of the claims of both, and to see in their missions the fulfillment of the Islamic prophecies.

ZOROASTRIANISM AND THE BAHAI MOVEMENT.

The present Zoroastrians, or Parsees, are but the remnant of a once powerful people. During the many vicissitudes of war and national decay their ancient political power has become dissipated, and through contact with peoples of other religions their original religious teaching has lost its purity, and a lifeless formalism has taken the place of its once vital spiritual force. As for the sacred literature of the Zoroastrians, it, like themselves, is now but fragmentary; the elements necessary to give it complete comprehensive form are lost.

Although many connecting links are missing in Zoroastrian holy writ, nevertheless its *spirit* is clear and apparent. Zoroaster taught a pure monotheism and the future existence and immortality of the soul, all of which He explained to the people in familiar terms and parables. The physical sun, which is the source of all physical life, He used as the symbol for the sun of truth, the manifestation of God, the source of all spiritual life, while the stars symbolized the lesser prophets. Purity is a fundamental teaching in Zoroastrianism. Both spiritual and physical purity are taught in its laws and ordinances, which were given in terms couched to meet the need of mankind in that ancient day. Fire being the great cleanser, it is the emblem used to denote spiritual purity, for it is through the spiritual fire of the love of God that men's souls are purified and quickened into eternal life. Zoroaster is pictured as bringing down from heaven the divine fire with which to purify mankind. The spiritual meaning of this is apparent, although for centuries the understanding of these truths was lost and the people ignorantly adhered to the *outer forms,* worshipping the sun, the stars and fire, hence the terms applied to them, "Sun and Fire Worshippers".

The same idea of resurrection or quickening, spiritual judgment and The Kingdom of God on earth, expressed in other religious teachings, are found in Zoroastrianism. The end of the Zoroastrian dispensation, it was foretold in their sacred literature, would be characterized by spiritual impurity, therefore the need of another manifestation to bring to earth the divine fire of the love of God for the purification of all people. The teaching has a number of prophecies regarding the coming of the great Latter-Day Prophet, spoken of as Shah Bahram, and the purification of the people of the earth by fire— the fire of the spirit.

The expectation of this coming of the prophet is symbolized in the Zoroastrian worship, when the people turn to worship to the rising sun. As the same physical sun rises and sets again and again, giving life to the earth, so does the sun of God's truth rise in each prophetic day and through the personality of the prophet of that day gives life to the souls which receive the rays of its spiritual warmth and power.

The Zoroastrians who are now hearing of the message of the Bahai Movement are realizing that it is the fulfillment of the prophecies and the spirit of their own religion, and through this teaching they are coming into touch with kindred spirits in all the world. Thus they are arising to perform their service in this great work of uniting all men in the love of The Kingdom.

HINDUISM AND THE BAHAI MOVEMENT.

The origin of Hinduism (Brahmanism), on account of the lack of annals and records in its literature, is practically lost to history. As it now is, Hinduism is a most complex system of philosophical thought, manners and customs. It lacks that unity of spirit and of form which the teaching originally possessed. In all religious systems men's ideas have gradually replaced the inspired wisdom of the founders. In Hinduism this is particularly true, so much so that it is only with the greatest difficulty that the original spirit and teaching can be traced. Even some of the most learned students of Hindu philosophy, have doubted that originally Hinduism was a revealed teaching, for since its sacred books contain no chronicles, the personalities of the revealers have been lost.

Of the *truth* in the original Hindu teachings, however, there is no doubt, for the voice of *the Spirit,* the source of all religion, speaks yet today through its holy books, the Vedas, despite the lapse of time since they were written.

According to the teaching in the most ancient of the Hindu sacred books, God the creator, is all in all, beside whom there is none other. Sacrifice is taught as the means of attaining nearness to God. Material sacrifice is the symbol for the sacrifice of all worldly desires and passions which separate men's souls from God, the highest attainment being that perfect at-onement with God which the giving up of every desire and passion alone can bring. Since God only is all in all, only *the life in Him* can be without change or end. This is eternal life.

The teaching in its original purity was a simple monotheism. The divine spirit spoke to the people through the mediumship of different personalities at different times. These inspired souls arose as the need for their teachings became evident among men, to whom they were sent as spiritual guides.

This thought is most clearly expressed in one of the Hindu sacred books, the "Bhagavad-Gita" or *the Lord's Song,* in which it is written, "Whenever there is decay of righteousness and there is exaltation of unrighteousness, then I

Myself come forth. For the protection of the good, for the destruction of evil doers, for the sake of firmly establishing righteousness, I am born from age to age. The foolish disregard Me when clad in human semblance, ignorant of My supreme nature, the great Lord of beings." The Hindus have here the promise of the coming of a great incarnation, Krishna, to occur in *this day*. He was to arise and establish universal righteousness and destroy spiritual ignorance or sin.

The latter-day Krishna was to lead the people back to the spirit of pure teaching as given by His predecessors, (former manifestations of the spirit of the Lord) and through spiritual wisdom and power was to overcome all unrighteousness establishing in its place spiritual enlightenment. Those illumined Hindus whom the Bahai cause is reaching see in Baha'o'llah the incarnation of the *spirit of God* and they accept him as their promised one, Krishna.

Thus, the Bahai teaching confirms the Hindu in the fundamental truth of his own religion, and it frees him from the superstition and caste which have for centuries kept his people in a state of both spiritual and physical bondage. Under this influence he attains to the real spirit of sacrifice as given in his ancient teachings, and to the real emancipation of the soul, which is in truth the fundamental tenet of the most ancient Hindus.

BUDDHISM AND THE BAHAI MOVEMENT.

Buddhism stands in the relation to Hinduism very much as Christianity does to Judaism. Chrisitanity sprang from Judaism as the mother religion, in like manner Buddhism came out from Hinduism. As Christianity and Judaism evolved two widely differing systems of philosophy, so have Buddhism and Hinduism evolved two theological systems, which not only do not resemble each other, but are in direct opposition. Jesus, the Christ, came not to destroy but to fulfill the law and prophets. Guatama, The Buddha, had no intention of departing from the true spiritual and original precepts of the teachings of Hinduism. His mission was to teach the people the divine significance of the past teachings, which had become to them but an empty form. Through Him millions of souls have received God's truth in the measure of their capacity, and according to the degree their condition demanded.

The Buddha taught of the one God, and of the life eternal. The state of nearness to God is termed *nirvana,* by the Buddhists. It is synonymous with the word heaven as used in the holy writings of other religions. Gautama wrote no books. The events of His life, and His words and teachings were recorded by His disciples and have been handed down to the people of succeeding generations.

Of the original teachings of The Buddha much has been lost, and replaced by the doctrines and beliefs of men who came after Him. In fact the latter-day Buddhist teachings, so rich in the ramifications and speculations of philosophical thought, bear about as much resemblance to the original spiritual teachings of The Buddha, as the present day multiplicity of creeds of any one of the world religions bears to the real teachings of its founder.

The Buddhists, like the Bahais, consider all religions to be, from the spiritual standpoint, one religion. They are without religious prejudice. They welcome all high elevating thought and teaching irrespective of its source. They believe Gautama, The Buddha, to have been one of a series of inspired souls sent to the peoples of various ages for divine training and guidance. As there were Buddhas who preceded Him, so there would be Buddhas who would succeed Him. They expect the coming of Maitrêya, or the great Fifth Buddha, whose coming, according to their traditions, is now due. His work is to be with all mankind and through Him the earthly conditions of the past are to change and be replaced by an age of divine wisdom and understanding.

The following excerpt from the recorded teachings of Gautama to His disciple Ananda, given just previous to His death, explains in a few words much of his teaching, "I am not the first Buddha who came upon earth, nor shall I be the last. I came to teach you the truth, and I have founded upon earth The Kingdom of Truth. Gautama Siddhârtha will die, but Buddha will live, for Buddha is the truth and the truth cannot die. He who believes in the truth and lives in it is My disciple, and I shall teach him. The religion which I have preached to you will flourish so long as my disciples cling to the truth, and lead a life of purity. In due time another Buddha will arise, and He will reveal to you the selfsame eternal truth which I have taught you". Ananda said: "How shall we know Him?" Gautama replied: "He will be known as Maitrêya, which means,'He whose name is Kindness'."

MODERN THOUGHT AND THE BAHAI MOVEMENT

During the past sixty or seventy years so-called "Modern Thought" has entered into the fold of every religion, preparing the people for a broad, universal conception of God's truth, a conception unfettered by the mental limitations of past ages. Although it is called "Modern

Thought," it is in reality the most ancient thought, for it is the resurrection of the spirit which the religions originally possessed, and which during so many centuries was lost to humanity.

Modern Thought has been as a plough, which has prepared the religious ground of the world to receive the spiritual seeds of The Kingdom. Modernism has uprooted ancient creed and dogma, and along with this uprooting, the faith of many has been shaken and much spiritual seeking has resulted. Now the Bahai teaching is sowing the seeds of a live faith in men's souls. It is demonstrating to the world that faith, religion and spirituality are vital and necessary forces in the world of humanity, and that they have nothing in common with the superstitions and imaginations of the past. The Modern Thoughtists of all races and religions are teaching the same principles as held by the followers of the Bahai cause. They realize that humanity as a whole is now passing through a period of spiritual rebirth, and this is the beginning of the age of spiritual wisdom, which is the millennium. In the great spiritual organism of the universe, the various parts and members are organically united and linked together as are the organs of the body. As there have been great changes and upheavals in the evolution of the material world, due to material causes, so there have been great phases of change and development in the evolution of the spiritual world, due to the action of spiritual causes.

The present day awakening, as seen in all of the many branches of Modern Thought, and the coming of another revelation are the direct result of certain great changes taking place in the spiritual realm of existence, which are being produced by spiritual causes. In the early morning when the sun is yet below the horizon, the heavens are illumined by its rays and the coming of day is evident to all. As the sun slowly rises, those upon the high places first see it, later those in the valleys see it also; and when it is at its zenith the whole country is receiving its rays and basking in its warmth.

So it is when the sun of truth manifests here upon earth for the guidance of the people. The manifestation or revelator, is preceded by the signs of spiritual awakening, which show the people that a new spiritual day or era is at hand. Those illumined souls of high spiritual discernment first recognize in the revealer or prophet, the source of the light of God; later, the people in general awaken to His spiritual power and wisdom and finally, through His teaching, both material and spiritual bounties are forthcoming to the world.

This wave of modernism which has swept over the world, dispelling the night of spiritual ignorance and superstition, is the first twilight of the great day of God upon earth. Already many illumined souls are seeing in the inspired revealers of the Bahai religion the light of the world to be and its point of diffusion. Later on, the whole world will realize that which now only the few see. Then, all humanity will be the recipients in full of the much anticipated bounties of The Kingdom of God upon the earth.

Resumé.

As the people of the various religions come into the spirit of the Bahai Cause, their faith in the truth of their own religion is augmented rather than lessened, for the spirit of this present day teaching is the same as that which actuated the early fathers of the ancient religions.

The Bahai Movement teaches *severance*. In his heart man must be severed from the world and its passions. His dependence must be upon God though outwardly he must live in the world, there fulfilling his material mission in life.

In the Bahai life, severance is comprised in the rebirth of the Christian, the spirit of obedience of the Jew, the submission of the Moslem, the purification of the Zoroastrian, the sacrifice of the Hindu, the renunciation of the Buddhist, and the "living in harmony with the divine" of the Modern Thoughtist. In the Bahai movement, is summed up all of the spiritual essence of the religions of the past, which is now given in a form most applicable to the present day needs of man, and adequate to cope with the modern universal problems.

IIV.
THE BAHAI SACRED WRITINGS
The Bab.

The book of The Bab, or His collective writings, is known as "The Beyan". That the mission of The Bab was introductory to the advent of Baha'o'llah is most clearly stated in this book, in which the coming of "Him whom God shall manifest" is the one great theme. In it The Bab exhorts the people spiritually to prepare themselves to meet and to recognize and to adhere to, Baha'o'llah when He should appear. He left certain laws and ordinances for the guidance of His followers until the advent of Baha'o'llah, all of which should be abrogated, with the promised coming. These writings, calculated to meet and minister to the local conditions which were chiefly Islamic, have as yet not been translated into English.

Baha'o'llah.

The writings of Baha'o'llah are numerous and are in general, comparatively brief treatises. Of these a number have been translated and published in the Occidental languages, while others still remain in the original Persian and Arabic texts.

One of the first books translated and published in English was the *Kitabu 'l-Ighan* (The Book of Assurance). This was written by Baha'o'llah during His exile in Baghdad, and was a reply to certain theological questions asked by a learned Mussulman divine. While the expression is couched in terms peculiar to Islamic thought, yet, deeper than these terms, are revealed universal spiritual teachings the essence of which appeals to the people of any religion.

In the Book of Assurance, Baha'o'llah quotes familiar texts from the Old and New Testaments of the Bible, and from the Koran of Mohammed, and He explains the spiritual truths contained in these three books, relative to the end and passing of the old dispensations, the coming of the Messiah, and the ushering into existence of the new dispensation of The Kingdom upon earth. He demonstrates the oneness of the teachings of the Jewish, Christian and Mussulman Holy literature regarding this Latter-Day advent of the Lord.

In the *Suratu'l Hykl* (Chapter upon the Temple or Body) Baha'o'llah treats of His calling, His arising in response thereto, and His mission here among men.

In The Book of the *Seven Valleys,* Baha'o'llah explains the different stages of the spiritual progress or development of the soul of man. These stages He divides into seven, which He terms "Valleys". This book was written to elucidate certain truths from the standpoint of Mysticism. In order to appreciate it, one must understand and be in sympathy with the spirit and teachings of the Mystics.

In the *Lawhu'l-Akdas* (The Holy Tablet) Baha'o'llah explains His cause to the Christian world. He demonstrates that now is the time of the end spoken of by Jesus, The Christ, and He exhorts the Christians to consider the importance of *this day* and of *its cause*. He demonstrates the necessity for relinquishing dependence upon the creeds and customs of the past ages, and exhorts all to adhere to the pure truth of the words of Jesus which, when understood, will confirm the truth revealed again in this day.

The Hidden Words (in two parts, one translated from the original Arabic text and the other from the Persian) contain the essence of the spiritual truths revealed by the divine revelators of the past. In these utterances the fundamental divine truths are again revealed to humanity in terms applicable to the exigencies of this age. Each verse is replete with spiritual significances, and in each is hidden a message, or word, for the hungry soul.

The Tablets of *Tarazat, Tajalleyat* and *Ishrakat,* contain exhortations regarding the conduct of man. In these books Baha'o'llah dwells upon those virtues, through the practice of which spiritually awakened man will evolve and attain to the state of nearness to God.

In the *Kitabu'l-Akdas* (Book of the Law) Baha'o'llah outlines both the material and spiritual laws for the guidance of the people of the coming dispensation. He provides for governmental laws based upon divine laws. These laws are not arbitrary. They are given with divine wisdom and their virtue will become apparent as men live in accordance with their statutes, for through so doing, the source of the ills of the day will disappear. The ordinances of the Bahai cause aim at the eradication of wrong-doing rather than the chastisement of those who perpetrate wickedness.

The *Kitabu'l-Ahd* (Book of the Testament) is the will and testament of Baha'o'llah to His followers. In this document He provides for the guidance of His followers after His passing, by appointing His beloved son, Abdul-Baha, to be the Center of His Covenant, towards whom all of the faithful should turn.

Baha'o'llah left many other writings to the world. These are, for the greater part, in the form of epistles or "Tablets," written to individuals. Noteworthy among these are the "Epistles to the Kings", written just previous to His arrival at Akka, and sent from this prison to all parts of the world, during His incarceration.

In these Tablets Baha'o'llah declares His Cause to the kings and potentates of the earth, exhorting them to turn to The Kingdom and to The Promised One whom God had sent to establish peace upon earth, to abolish warfare, and to give their attention to the establishment of those institutions which would benefit their subjects.

Abdul-Baha

The writings of Abdul-Baha are for the greater part epistles ("Tablets") written to individuals, or to assemblies of the followers. These are explanatory of the revealed writings of Baha'o'llah. A number of Abdul-Baha's lessons upon various spiritual subjects have been collected, translated and published by one of his followers, under the title of *"Some Answered Questions"*. This work is of value to the student who desires an insight into the spirit of the teaching. Abdul-Baha's mission is that of amplifying and applying the truth as revealed by his father. This, Abdul-Baha is accomplishing by his life of service and example even more than by his words. His Life is his book. From him is proceeding that power of understanding which is enabling his followers to realize and to attain to the spiritual admonitions of Baha'o'llah.

In reading the translations of the writings of The Bäb, Baha'o'llah and Abdul-Baha, the westerner should always bear in mind two things: 1st, these original writings were in the symbolic and florid style of the Persian or Arabic tongues, many of the expressions and similes of which are untranslatable and, perforce, have been rendered literally, consequently much of the rich poetic oriental expression is out of harmony with the more matter-of-fact occidental tongue, through which, in translation, it is forced to express itself; 2d, many of these writings were sent to people in intellectual conditions foreign to those to which we are accustomed here in the west. The object of these teachers being to make spiritual connection with souls, they sometimes employ one line of thought and terminology, and sometimes another, from an entirely different point of view. For instance, in order to reach a Mussulman the argument must be Islamic, whereas to reach a Christian, it must be Christian, etc.

In studying these writings let the reader first familiarize himself with all the conditions under which they were written: the writer, the people to whom he was writing, their previous religious training, the tongue, etc.; then he will understand the spiritual wisdom of the writings, the truth of which will not be obscured by expression, names or terminology.

VIII.
SOCIAL REFORMS, LAWS, AND ORDINANCES

Not only did Baha'o'llah reveal spiritual laws and principles for the people of the world, but He also outlined social reforms for the more material guidance and well-being of mankind.

The spiritual or religious foundation is the essential foundation; social reforms are the fruit of spiritual growth. Up to the present time but few of the proposed institutions of the Bahai faith have been established. Now is the time for spiritual seed sowing, later will come the time of spiritual fruitage and harvest. Now the believers are establishing the spiritual institutions of the teachings, spreading the message, enkindling faith and love in men's hearts. The future will see materialized the fruit of the labors of the Bahais of today when, added to the present development of the movement, will be all the institutions to round out the work, thus accomplishing the complete design, as outlined by Baha'o'llah.

The Ordinances of the Bahai faith are in accord with the natural laws governing human relations and affairs, and are so ordered as to bring forth the highest and most perfect physical, moral and spiritual development of all who place themselves within the sphere of influence. These laws are to be followed by the people from choice, not by compulsion. As people know and understand the wisdom of the precepts of Baha'o'llah, they will from volition, and for their own welfare and that of those about them, desire to live according to His advice.

Perfect liberty and freedom in religious thought and belief is to be allowed every one.

The Bahais are exhorted to mingle freely with people of all creeds, and in no way to shut themselves off from those of other beliefs. Neither should they criticise nor denounce the teachings nor the followers of other religious movements. Through fraternal intercourse, kindness, and loving service to all humanity, the believers in this *latter-day revelation* will eventually demonstrate its truth to all the world.

While the Bahais are commanded not to interfere with the religion of others, other people are advised to relinquish those creeds and customs which separate them into many divisions, in order that all may come into the one great spiritual unity of The Kingdom. All things find their birth in unity. The life of any being or organization of beings is dependent upon this principle. Therefore, how important is unity, and of the various kinds how all-important is spiritual and religious unity, for it is the foundation of all unity and of the progress of the world.

With the development of the spiritual world-unity, Baha'o'llah anticipated various universal institutions for the great benefit of humanity. He exhorted the rulers and governments of the world to abolish warfare and establish peace; to settle international difficulties by arbitration rather than by bloodshed. In order to facilitate international understanding and unite all people, Baha'o'llah advocated a universal language, which would itself be instrumental in the promotion of mutual understanding and sympathy between peoples.

From Baha'o'llah's writings, it does not seem to have been His idea that the kings of this earth should cease to exist, but rather that all governments should be established upon a system of representation, without which no government can uphold the rights of the people. The followers of Baha should be law-abiding citizens in whatever country they may dwell and they should be loyal supporters of all just and righteous governments.

One of the institutions of The Bab was the rearrangement of the calendar. This change was confirmed by Baha'o'llah, and the new calendar is beginning to be used by Bahais. Eventually it will supersede the many systems now current. The Bahai Era begins with the year 1844 A. D. or 1260 A. H. The first day of the Bahai year falls on March 21st, the day upon which the sun enters the sign of Aries, and is commonly known as the first day of spring. The year is divided into nineteen months of nineteen days each, making in all 361 days to which are added four (every fourth year five) intercalary days, to complete the 365 or 366 days of the year.

The Bahais have nothing in their own religion to exclude those holding different views. They have no form of membership, no formulated creed nor institutions to differentiate them outwardly from other people. Their work is ever inward rather than outward, and for the benefit of all rather than a few. In this religion there is no priesthood. Teaching is given without money and without price. All are teachers, each in his own sphere of life. Those, able and fitted to do so, go forth as speakers, while others teach quietly by their deeds, and by speaking the message when they find a hearer. While the cause asks only for the hearts of its followers, nevertheless, when the heart is in the work there comes the desire to give and to do something material for the movement. The giving of tithes for carrying on the Bahai work is a privilege, not an obligation.

Baha'o'llah, like all of the world's religious teachers, laid great stress upon prayer and fasting. Both are necessary for the development of the soul. Through prayer the soul is brought into communion with God and receives the spiritual sustenance necessary for its life and well-being. Through fasting the soul becomes freed from the materiality of the flesh; it then apprehends higher things, becomes conscious of divine realities, and receives the spiritual life forces to a higher degree than possible under the normal condition of the body.

Baha'o'llah clearly states that seeking refuge in creed and dogma, and faith without works, are not acceptable. The Bahais have no forms or ceremonials, such as have characterized the religions of the past. Prayer is made individually by the suppliant to God. Prayer, supplemented by a pure and useful life in this world, forms the elements of true worship. Every one should have an occupation, which conduces to the welfare of humanity, the diligent pursuance of which is in itself an act of worship.

The Bahai teaching encourages marriage, while asceticism and celibacy are discouraged. Monogamy is taught, and among the believers in the Orient is gradually replacing the systems of polygamy which have always existed there. The body should be developed, not mortified, because it is the medium through which the spirit works. A good and perfect body is desirable.

The executive affairs of the Bahai cause will eventually be presided over by a synod, known as the "House of Justice". Its members will be selected by the people. These members are to be qualified by spiritual characteristics and wisdom. They will be the trustees of the people. Their mission will be to serve the people in the numerous avenues of Bahai activity, in charitable and philanthropic works, and all the practical institutions which make for the welfare of the people and the cause. The House of Justice will meet at stated times and in various parts of the world, for the performance of its work. In addition to this general or central House of Justice for all the world, there will be assemblages in each community for the carrying on of local service.

Baha'o'llah strongly denounced the taking of opium and kindred drugs. The Bahais do not use intoxicating liquors as beverages, and among them even the use of tobacco is discouraged. Gambling is forbidden, as having a demoralizing effect upon the people. In fact all excesses, tending to weaken the body and the moral force of man, should be eschewed by him.

Individual advancement and personal incentive are to be fostered and encouraged, but the general weal of the mass is even more to be considered. The weak and unfortunate ones are to be protected from the greedy ones. Profit in business is to be sought, but one person has no right to enrich himself at the expense of another. When the ordinances of Baha'o'llah are established there will be fewer extremes of wealth and poverty. The people will be better off than they are now. The Bahai cause is prepared to meet and to reform the many human ills which the humanitarian thinkers and workers of the day are striving to eradicate. This is being accomplished through the spiritualizing method of changing the natural hardness of men's hearts by infusing into them the Love of God.

In the Bahai cause woman holds a position equal to that of man. She is not denied any rights. Through the Bahai teaching the women in the oriental countries are already reaping the benefits of education and are advancing in many ways, which customs of their former religion would close to them. It is hardly necessary here to mention those laws touching upon hygiene and the education of both sexes, and the admonitions forbidding mendicity, slavery, cruelty to animals and other offences, because, though in the Orient the need for them is yet very great, our western civilization has already accomplished these reforms.

While religion and state will never be reunited upon the old lines of creed and dogma, the Bahais look forward to the time when the states, or governments of the nations, will be founded upon a spiritual foundation—when the material laws of men will be founded and enforced according to the principles of the divine laws of God. Religion is necessary to man. Nations, as well as individuals, have at times tried to live without religion and the results have always been disastrous. The divine foundation is the only foundation upon which to build any institution that shall endure. The ideal government rests upon this foundation, which is not a union of *church* and state, but a union of *religion* and state.

Eventually, in every Bahai center there will be a building (temple) set apart for The Lord's use. Grouped about this, as a center, will be various institutions for the benefit of man—hospitals, homes, hospices, colleges, and other philanthropic enterprises. All of these buildings together, will constitute the Mashrak-El-Azcar: (literally "The dawning place of the mentions of God").

The central building, or Temple proper, will be a nine-sided structure surmounted by a dome, and surrounded by gardens. The number 9 is symbolic of the Spirit of God Manifest. The Temple will be a sanctuary for the reading or chanting of the "Holy Words," for meditation and for prayer, a place of universal worship open to all, in which people of all races and religions can worship God individually, in spirit and in truth, without the intermediary of church, priest or ritual.

The practical institutions of the Mashrak-El-Azcar will afford the opportunity for the establishment in the world of all branches of those progressive works for which the Bahai cause stands. In this day, religion is to be the direct source of inspiration in all secular affairs. The Bahai faith stands as the promoter of advancement in every line of human activity and development, and therefore every phase of these innumerable activities will draw its life from, and be an integral part of, the Mashrak-El-Azcar. In the Bahai teaching one finds exhortations to prayer and worship, upon the one hand, and exhortations to work and service to humanity upon the other. "Faith without deeds is not acceptable," therefore the Bahai religious work includes all work and service needful to man. This faith stands for all material and social progress. This idea is developed in the Mashrak-El-Azcar.

The Mashrak-El-Azcar is the symbolic expression of the prophet or the manifestation of God. The central building or place of worship may be compared to the heart or the innermost point of illumination, while the surrounding institutions may be compared to the fruit of (or service and good works performed by) the manifestation. Within the house of worship the people will find their inspiration, while through the surrounding institutions they will manifest this inspiration to the world, by loving service to humanity.

Not long since, in the city of Eshkabad, in Russian Turkestan, such a Mashrak-El-Azcar was built. This work represents the combined efforts of the Bahais throughout the Orient. Its architectural beauty and size testify to the loving offerings of those believers, while the idea for which it stands is far above the conception of the surrounding people.

In this service, of the Mashrak-El-Azcar, as well as many others the Bahais are laying a foundation, of whose existence the world in general is now not aware, for the alleviation of many human evils. The people of the future will understand the far-sightedness of these people of to-day in their effort to bring all secular affairs under spiritual guidance.

The Bahais of the west are following in the steps of their oriental brethren. In the city of Chicago a movement has been started for the erection there of the first Mashrak-El-Azcar in the Occident. Already an extensive building site has been purchased, overlooking Lake Michigan, and it is hoped that soon the building will be begun. Offerings for this work have been sent from the Bahais in all parts of the world. The Mashrak-El-Azcar represents the sum total of all the Bahai activities. Abdul-Baha has repeatedly written to the believers in America, that of all works the building of the Mashrak-El-Azcar is the most important. It is the foundation for the new order of the spiritual Kingdom upon earth, therefore its importance cannot be overestimated. When it stands accomplished, it will be as a haven of rest to those who seek communion with God within its sacred precincts; while outwardly, it will be as a banner manifesting to the world the service and the purpose of the Bahai cause.

IX.
THE NEED OF THE TIMES

Living, spiritual religion is the cause of social reform. It precedes and is the leader of human progress, and is the basis of civilization. Lifeless religion, of theology and form, precedes and is the cause of social and moral degradation. It retards human progress, and is the destroyer of civilization. Live religion produces peace and harmony. Dead religion makes warfare and discord.

Each of the world's spiritual teachers was in advance of the people of his time. Each was independent of the thought and institutions of his day, and was a creator of thought, morals and social advancement. This progressive spirit characterized each of the great religious movements during its earlier days.

Later, religion ceased to be an independent institution (a leader of the people), and it became a dependent institution, dependent upon and catering to the thought of the people of the day. Its mission as a leader and a creator of thought and morals was at an end, and instead of elevating the people, it retarded their progress and became the cause of stagnation and disintegration. Advancing civilization has had no more subtle or persistent enemy to contend with than lifeless religious systems.

Foremost among the world problems of the day is the abolition of war and the establishment of Peace. National, racial and religious hatred have been the principal causes of warfare. The present different religious teachings or philosophies, not only are not working for Peace upon earth, but through their influence upon men are actually holding people at variance, dividing humanity, and in many cases have been the direct cause of war. Since the Bahai teaching is striking a fatal blow at these prejudices, it is not only eliminating the cause of strife, but, in place of this enmity, it is planting a virile and growing unity between all peoples.

The Bahai principle of unity is not merely negative, a suspension of inharmony, it is a positive force for unity, which, as it grows, transmutes destructive forces into constructive forces. It stands for, and is a promoter of, all of the universal progressive movements uniting nations, which the world now needs. Through it, the differences between eastern and western thought, manners and customs, and the lack of confidence between all people, are being changed and replaced by oneness of thought and action and by confidence and fraternity.

The Bahai Cause stands for:

The Unity of all Religions.

The Political Unity of nations.

The Social Unity of all classes, peoples and races.

The Unity of Languages in one universal language.

Universal Suffrage.

The Advancement of all Material Institutions, conducive to the general welfare of man; his enlightenment and progress.

World Peace.

All of which is to be established upon the foundation of spiritual unity between peoples.

In this day, the peoples of the world are being drawn together by all of the material forces of civilization. Commerce and political relations have brought people of all nations, races and religions together, upon the plane of their outer activities, but as yet they form a heterogenous mixture, having no inner or spiritual ground upon which to build a fundamental unity. Such a spiritual meeting ground of unity is now the most needed thing in the world. The time is at hand for the people of the world to unite in all matters, most of all in religion, since it is the most potent factor in shaping character. The good character of nations has been made by religion and it has been destroyed through the lack of it.

The theologies of the past have nothing to offer the world today as the solution of this mighty problem. Each of them was evolved under conditions of the past, and has no relation to, power or influence upon, the present universal world-needs.

The day of *dependent religion* is at an end, and this world is now ripe for the leadership of a virile religious movement: a religion ahead of the times, one whose teaching is independent of, and not limited by the current thought of man; that will lead the world onward, infusing into it the spiritual force to reform its institutions, and unite all races and nations, oriental and occidental, in faith in God and confidence in one another, thus making a firm spiritual foundation for the coming great world-civilization.

"The Bahai teaching is not an eclectic philosophy, neither is it a sect. *It is a living spiritual religion.* Because of its soul inspiring qualities, it appeals alike to the unschooled and the learned, to the masses and the few. The Bāb, Baha'o'llah and Abdul-Baha stand out as divine teachers and leaders, independent of the world's attitude and thought. They are not building a theological system from intellectual material. Like all world movers they were far ahead of their times. Peace, arbitration and an international language, in fact a universal civilization, were unthought of by the world, when these teachers, over a half century ago, announced their spiritual message, in which is incorporated the solution of all the teeming questions which now occupy the minds of some of the greatest thinkers and philanthropists of the age. Upon every hand people are clamoring to understand more clearly the principles of peace to which the Bahai leaders and their followers have borne witness by trials and suffering and death.

The Bahai cause is ministering to the great spiritual need of the day, by planting in the soul of the world a living religion of brotherhood. Because of this universal need, this cause is destined to grow until it envelops the whole world, uniting all men and leading them onward toward the age of spiritual enlightenment, prosperity, and peace.

X.
ORIENTAL-OCCIDENTAL UNITY.

The Orient can truly be said to be the mother of the human race. From her heart went forth those great racial wave movements which have peopled the earth. In her mountain fastnesses the prophets communed with God and received His life-giving truth (which has been the inspiration of all mankind), and in her valleys and upon her plains civilization had its dawn.

The Occident can with equal truth be said to be the son, or man-child of the mother Orient. Both materially and spiritually the Occident has received its physical life and its religious inspiration from the Orient, the fruit of which is the present occidental civilization.

During many centuries the peoples of the East and those of the West have been separated by barriers, racial, religious, geographic and political. So complete has been this segregation, that these two halves of humanity have developed along different lines of thought, manners and customs, until the very natures and characteristics of these peoples have become, in general, distinct and foreign to each other.

Now, in these latter days, through the breaking down of the former material barriers, the oriental and occidental peoples are being forced one upon the other. Through international relations, the increase of foreign commerce, and the travel and mingling of people, the Orientals and Occidentals are daily coming into closer relations upon the material plane of life. As yet, however, this is but a superficial mingling, void of any basic unity.

Without any trust, confidence or affinity for one another, the Oriental and Occidental are at variance in almost every way. That which will destroy this variance is the spiritual confidence, trust, and mutual affinity, which the Bahai faith is creating between the East and the West. Through the establishment of such practical institutions of service as will demonstrate this spiritual unity, the greatest material and spiritual benefit to all humanity will result, for, springing from this spiritual foundation will be all of those religious, political, and social activities, for which the Bahai cause stands, and which will eventually unite in one civilization all the peoples of the world.

The Bahai cause stands for spiritual unity manifested in every phase and activity of life. The Bab, Baha'o'llah and Abul-Baha stand pre-eminent as lovers and servants of humanity. Their mission was that of spiritual uniting and life giving, therefore their teachings influence every phase and detail of life. With the fruition of this cause, the great Orient-Occident problem will be solved. Through this Bahai spiritual unity encompassing all peoples, oriental and occidental characteristics will so blend that a new *world type of man* will be evolved: one which will embody, not only the present existing virtues of the East and the West, but most of all, the highest spiritual possibilities of humanity, which can come to light only as people unite and live according to divine law applied to every phase of life.

The stages of development through which collective man passes are parallel and analogous to those through which he passes as an individual. Until the state of physical maturity is reached, individual men and women are content to live apart from one another. Each is developing his or her own mental and physical characteristics, and, normally, two different and distinct types, masculine and feminine, are the result.

When maturity is reached, the reason for the difference in the characteristics of man and woman becomes apparent. Affinity and union take place between these differing natures and a great change is produced in each. One supplies what the other lacks, and two rounded out and more perfect lives is the result, and further, through this love union of man and woman, the way is made for the birth of other human beings. When two parents are united by the bonds of a complete love, their children come into this world under the highest possible auspices for both bodily and soul development, and in their natures are found magnified the combined virtues of both parents.

In this day, the human race is reaching the stage of maturity, the Orient along her own characteristic lines, and the Occident along his own characteristic lines. Now their future development depends upon their union, both spiritual and physical. These two halves of humanity, eastern and western, must unite and become as one in every respect, spiritual and material, in order that each may reach its highest development. From this union will come the future universal world-type of man, who will combine in himself all the human virtues and the highest spiritual possibilities.

Such an union between the East and West can never be accomplished upon any foundation other than a spiritual one. When the Occident and the Orient meet on a common spiritual ground, then an intellectual and social unity in all of its forms with all of its institutions, will result.

By brute force a man can dominate a woman while the souls of both are suffering, although neither may be aware of this condition. In the perfect marriage, neither the man nor the woman dominates the other. Through love, they become as one soul in two bodies. So must it be between the Occident and the Orient. Many oriental countries have been held by occidental nations through force. This has not been conducive in any way to the solution of this world problem. Under a regime of force, both peoples, the dominant and the dominated, suffer from lack of unity. Each remains within itself, its life forces and possibilities undeveloped, pent up, and suffering for lack of the expression which only the freedom of harmony can give.

In the coming epoch of religious, racial and national unity, for which the Bahai cause is paving the way, there will be no question of "supremacy" over one another. All peoples will be members of one harmonious world-family, each working to protect and help the other. Under this order, which is the order of God's Kingdom, the highest civic and national institutions will be evolved, and the masses of the people will attain to a high state of spiritual, moral and physical development. Thus, humanity will attain to a state of civilization and advancement, of the greatness of which no one can now form any conception.

XI.
ETERNAL LIFE

Eternal life is the condition of the spiritually alive or divinely quickened soul.

To be merely alive to physical, animal and human things is not life according to religious terminology. To be alive in the spiritual sense is to be conscious of the Spirit of God manifest, to believe in Him, and to do according to His will. The soul is an indestructible entity which exists after its separation or freedom from the material body. Yet mere natural existence, either here or in the life beyond, is not life from the spiritual or divine view-point.

Through "The Manifestation," the soul of natural man is quickened with divine or eternal life, which is as a new and a higher dimension added to his human nature. By virtue of this divine quickening, the spiritually-born soul comes directly under divine guidance. Though in the world, yet it lives in a higher realm than before —the divine realm—from which it receives life, and a force that characterizes it with higher qualities. Thus, through the baptism of the spirit or the Word of God revealed, the soul passes from the condition of natural darkness into one of divine light, from the condition of spiritual ignorance or death, into that of spiritual awakeness or eternal life.

Eternal life is not a condition to which the soul attains through its own virtue or through evolution from the natural plane. It is a gift and a bounty from God bestowed upon natural man through Revelation. It is given through God's mercy and favor, not through His justice. There is evolution upon the natural plane, confined to that plane, and also evolution upon the spiritual plane, confined to that plane, but there is no evolution from one plane to the other. In the Divine Kingdom, before as well as after death, there is progression towards perfection of the type of perfect spiritual manhood. There is nothing to which the soul may evolve beyond perfect spiritual manhood, for spiritual man is the highest being of God's creation, above which there is no creation. Male and female are conditions of the physical realm and not of the spiritual kingdom. By virtue of the Holy Spirit, manifesting through the revealer, the souls of His followers are lifted from the lower to the higher plane, from natural manhood to spiritual manhood, they become characterized with divine qualities, and they show forth in their lives the fruits of the Spirit.

As metal is heated in the fire and so partakes of the characteristics of the fire until it is like the fire, so the soul, through the revealed word, becomes characterized by divine characteristics. As with the metal, the source of the heat being outside of it, the moment it is removed from the fire it loses the characteristics of the fire, so it is with the human soul, for when it separates itself from God's Word, divine characteristics cease to emanate from it. The source of divine life is not in man but in The Word revealed, and of man's divine enlightenment, in his dependence upon The Word.

Good actions and good deeds characterize the quickened soul, but good actions and good deeds are not in themselves a proof that a soul is divinely quickened. Many souls without faith or spiritual assurance lead exemplary lives from the ethical standard, while, upon the other hand, many souls sunken in crime and depravity become touched by the spirit and are born into The

Kingdom, and bring forth the fruits of the divine life.

Life in its highest and fullest sense, exists in that soul in which all of the life forces, both divine and material, reach their highest development. Neither a physically perfect man nor a highly educated man is upon the highest plane until he is quickened, and alive to the divine realities. The perfect type of manhood has an all-round physical, psychical, intellectual and divinely spiritual development. As souls are dedicated to God's service and become cleansed and pure from earthly conditions, then the deepest mysteries of The Kingdom become clear to them. All doubts and fears are dispelled by faith and assurance, while all inharmonious conditions are replaced by harmonious ones through the love of God burning in the soul. This is Eternal Life.

XII.
HEAVEN AND HELL.

Heaven and hell, salvation and sin, light and darkness, are terms employed to differentiate the two spiritual conditions of the soul of man.

The spiritually quickened soul, alive with the life of the Spirit, is that condition called heaven, while the unawakened soul, not yet conscious of the bounty of God, nor alive in His Spirit, is that state of spiritual lethargy or darkness called hell. These two conditions apply to the life of the soul in this world, as to the soul in the great beyond. As there are conditions of both spiritual awakeness and spiritual slumber here in this life, so there are these same conditions in the realm of the immaterial into which the soul passes upon leaving this body.

God's mercy is never wearied. As for those souls who go out into the great beyond without being spiritually awakened here, for their quickening He has ways and means unknown to us. Reward and punishment are of two kinds, natural and spiritual. In the world of nature every good act, in accord with her laws, produces a good effect, and every violation of nature's principles has a harmful, or detrimental effect upon the individual. The reward and punishment, the good or the bad effect following the good or bad action of man, is inevitable; it is according to fixed law. Likewise, according to the divine law he advances spiritually, and when he violates that law he suffers spiritually. Spiritual conditions, however, are more far reaching than material conditions, for they are not limited to this earthly plane; they are eternal.

The greatest blessing which can descend upon

man is the knowledge of God. The greatest calamity is to be deprived of this knowledge. Through God's mercy He has given man the blessing of knowing Him. He has also given man free will to accept or reject this blessing as he wills, therefore divine knowledge or ignorance comes to man, as reward or punishment for his choice.

A soul in this world may reject the light and be spiritually deprived, and at the same time be totally ignorant of its state of deprivation. From the spiritual view-point a soul may be in darkness and in spiritual torment, but because of the lack of spiritual perception this soul may not realize its own condition.

As darkness is but the absence of light, so ignorance is but the absence of knowledge, and spiritual death but the absence of spiritual life. Evil has no life nor positive existence. It is negative, it is the absence of positive light. Thus darkness, ignorance and death are negative and have no power within themselves, while light, knowledge and life are positive powers, containing those elements which dispel their opposites.

As there are many degrees of spiritual enlightenment for the soul while it inhabits the physical body, so are there many degrees for it in the realms beyond this world. In this world man is endowed with the freedom of choice. When Divine Grace is offered him, he can accept or reject it as he chooses. Thus, his responsibility is great. Choice between light and darkness—divine illumination and ignorance exists, however, here in this world only. In the realms beyond, these earthly conditions do not exist. There the soul can exercise no free choice, as only the good exists. There, spiritual progress and development are also possible, but do not depend upon the *will of the individual,* but wholly upon the mercy and bounty of God. It is only in this life that man can *voluntarily* choose to accept the life of the Spirit and through *this choice* attain to divine blesings.

The Kingdom of Heaven is, both here and hereafter, for those souls who are alive in The Lord. Through revelation the divine promise has been extended to man at various times through the ages, that in the fullness of time the quickening spirit of The Lord, through the Latter-Day Messiah, would be so poured out upon all men of all races, that the vast majority of mankind would be illumined and quickened and be in the state called heaven. The past conditions of spiritual ignorance and darkness would pass, and the day of divine wisdom, or great age would come. The "end of the world," "the destruction of the world," and similar terms used in holy writ, are symbolic of the end of the ages of spiritual darkness and sin, and the ushering into existence of the new epoch of general spiritual illumination. The coming age of peace, prosperity, and divine enlightenment will be The Kingdom of God upon earth.

The Kingdom hereafter, is that state of life in which the spiritually illumined souls find themselves after passing from the physical body. Man's objective senses, being of the plane of this natural realm, convey to the mind only conceptions of conditions peculiar to this material world, therefore, of that immaterial condition of the soul in the existence beyond this world, man can form no mental conception whatever. As the soul attains to a greater and fuller divine life, it becomes conscious and is assured of the perpetuity and eternalness of the state of awakening, and has no doubt as to the reality of the life eternal, yet can not form a mental conception of that condition because it is beyond the scope of man's imagination.

Before the physical birth of the child into this world, it is developing its physical organs, the utility of which do not become apparent until birth. During its pre-natal life, through the mother, the child is nourished by life forces from the world into which it is to be born.

So it is with the spiritual life of the soul. While in this body, the soul is developing spiritual virtues and faculties, the need for, and virtue of which do not now appear, but which will become apparent when it enters into the life beyond. Again like the child, the soul, while in this body, is spiritually nourished with force from that realm or condition into which it will be born or enter, upon leaving its prior condition.

The Bahai believes that, while so-called death in a sense separates souls for a time, there is a spiritual link binding all together. The souls in the realm beyond, retain remembrance of things here, as well as of those near to them. Through intercession there, souls here are helped. All quickened souls are spiritually united. This tie is eternal. It is not dependent upon physical means. All souls, born of the spirit, are different members of one great spiritual body, and whether those members are on this earth or in the realm beyond, there is a connection between them which death does not sever. Natural ties are severed when the soul leaves the body, but spiritual ties are eternal. Through the sincere prayers of others a soul is helped while here in this world, and likewise, through the intercession of others, a soul having passed from this life is helped on his spiritual way in the realm beyond;

for progress is not confined to this earthly existence. The souls, too, who have passed on, are able through their intercessions to help those here on earth. All of this is possible because the pervading spirit of God is uniting the souls of The Kingdom at all times and under all conditions.

XIII.
SCIENCE AND RELIGION.

Natural or material science is classified knowledge of the human, animal, vegetable and mineral kingdoms; religion, or spiritual science, is classified knowledge of the life of the spiritual, or divine kingdom, and the laws which govern it. There is no inharmony nor conflict between these two realms, for there is perfect accord throughout the whole of God's creation. Natural science teaches men how to live properly upon this human plane. Through observing its laws and living in accord with them, man attains to a high state of material, physical, psychic, and intellectual development. On the other hand, the prophets have revealed to humanity the laws which govern the spiritual kingdom of souls. As people live in accord with these divine laws, their souls develop spiritually and they attain to a high state of general development, for with the spiritual development, follows an evolution in the natural or material development of man. When men understand the realities of both the natural and divine realms, they will find no conflict between religion and science.

The reason that science and religion have contended in the past, with each other, is because religious teachings have contained so many imaginations and superstitions as to make them inpossible of acceptance to men of science. To be sure, these superstitions did not exist in the purity of the teachings as given by the prophets themselves. Superstitions are the impediments which religion has gathered as it has been handed down through the ages. Science finds only this dross a contradiction of her knowledge, but the spiritual teachings, though they deal with a higher realm, are in perfect accord with natural science.

The Bahai teaching is logical and reasonable. It is free from superstition and is compatible with modern science. There is in it spiritual force, which is its very life and essence. This transcends mere intellect, logic and reason, although it is in perfect accord and harmony with them.

One great work which the Bahai cause is accomplishing is the harmonizing of science and religion. It shows scientific people that true religion not only is not opposed to science, but that it is itself scientific, and that man needs more than mere intellectual food—he needs spiritual knowledge. Not until man adds the spiritual to the intellectual has he that perfect balance, by virtue of which he attains to highest development. The Bahai teaching is bringing a stronger, firmer and more vital faith into the religious world. Through the spirit of this movement, people of the old established religions realize that they have nothing to fear from the world of modern scientific thought. Under this influence, the old superstitions are dropping away, but the pure, untarnished truth is standing supreme.

The realization that there is no conflict between the material and divine realms, that material truth and divine truth are in perfect accord, frees man from superstition and fear, and gives him faith and assurance, opening before him the door to the highest possibilities and development.

XIV.
THE SUPERNATURAL

Miracles form no part of the Bahai teaching.

The prophets were endowed with powers, both natural and spiritual, through which they accomplished that which was impossible to ordinary man. The unusual things which they did were for the instruction and education and spiritual quickening of those about them. The miracles ascribed to them have been a great test of faith for the people of after generations, for to many, miracles are not a proof of divinity.

A material phenomenon seemingly outside the domain of natural law, would not prove to thinking people that the doer was divine. In these days of physical and psychological experiment and research no one would ascribe divine powers to the physicist or the psychologist who astonished the world with discoveries and demonstrations.

Many wonderful things are recorded by the Bahais, illustrative of the spiritual powers of the founders of their religion, but these form no part of the teaching nor are they ever mentioned as *proofs,* for, if so, they would prove a stumbling block rather than an attraction to truth seekers.

The great and wonderful miracle, performed by the prophets and manifestations of the past and the present, is their power to implant in the souls of men the love of God, to quicken humanity with divine life and, with all of the earthly forces against them, to accomplish their divine work. This is a real, a spiritual miracle.

XV.
EDUCATIONAL ASPECT OF THE BAHAI TEACHING.

In order to produce world unity, the superstitions and prejudices of past ages must be removed from men's minds. Lack of education, creates narrowness and prejudice; education, brings broadness of view, and sympathy with others.

The past systems of narrow education have tended more towards perpetuating than eradicating inharmony between men. The followers of the different religious systems, being at variance with one another, have in their educational systems handed down to coming generations the prejudice, ignorance and dogmatism of past generations, thus instilling into the children all the soul-retarding elements which encumbered the natures of the parents. The natural tendency of man has been to remain upon the old level of inharmony rather than to arise therefrom by his own will.

Now, in this enlightened age, there has appeared in the world simultaneously with the Bahai revelation, a new order of educational methods. Former dogma and prejudice are no longer taught to children, and the minds of the youths of this generation are not thus limited and handicapped.

In fact, in this day, in freeing our educational system from the superstition, prejudice and dogma of the past, the mistake has been made of eliminating, also, all spiritual precepts from the general instruction of children. Thinking educators are beginning to see the demoralizing results of the lack of spiritual instruction in the present system; for in the people of this generation is manifest, to an alarming degree, the inroads of certain vices against which they are unable to protect themselves because of the want of moral and spiritual training and poise.

It is an all-round education, for which the Bahai cause stands. Man is a combination of several natures and his general well-being depends upon a balanced training and development. Bodily he must train and develop his physical powers in order to have a good and perfect organism through which to manifest the higher man. Physically and mentally he must train and develop the powers of perception, memory and reason, that he may have mental organism through which to manifest the higher spiritual man. Man's spiritual training and soul development is the most important of all education. This is the highest and greatest power within his being; therefore its importance cannot be overestimated. By religious and spiritual training is not meant the teaching of doctrine or creed, but rather, inculcating into man the knowledge of the Truth.

When man has attained to the Bahai conception of education, he is indeed educated in every sense of the word. This is the only education which fully fits man for the life here, as well as for the life hereafter.

The Bahai teaching stands for the higher education of woman. In some recent instructions sent to the Orient, Abdul-Baha has exhorted the Bahais to give their daughters every possible educational advantage, telling them it was even more necessary that their girls should be educated than their boys, because women are the mothers and the natural teachers of men, and it is of the greatest importance to the race that they be highly educated. Already several Bahai women physicians and nurses are working in Persia. Their work is of the greatest importance among the women, because they are able to penetrate into the seclusion of the family life of the people, in ways not open to men.

Several other Americans, Bahais, have gone to Persia as teachers, and are associated there with the educational work. Quite recently a girls' school was opened by the Bahais in Teheran, and from the last accounts, there were more scholars than could be accommodated. In addition to this, educational work is being carried on in all of the oriental countries, where there are congregations of Believers. Each year brings Bahai students to Europe and America, who after completing their studies return to their own countries as teachers.

Through liberal education and the diffusion of knowledge and wisdom, both spiritual and material, the superstitions and limitations of the past will cease to exist, all people will be in sympathy with humanity as a whole, and each individual will consider himself a citizen of the world rather than exclusively of one country, and one people.

XVI.
THE BAHAI MOVEMENT AND THE ECONOMIC QUESTIONS OF THE DAY.

With the expansion of civilization and the peopling of the world, the field for conquest is so rapidly diminishing that already a great change has been produced in the economic conditions of the world. Owing to the present international conditions, and the nearness of nations, war is assuming an aspect more detrimental to all parties than it has ever had in the past. Arbitration must in the end supplant national conquest and warfare.

Likewise, the warlike methods upon which the world's commerce has been conducted will ere long become obsolete, because of the passing of the conditions which made those methods possible. Commercial relations are now becoming so intimate between nations, that co-operation must eventually take the place of the present warfare of illegitimate competition, in the business world.

The Bahai cause teaches co-operation in all affairs. Through working together for the good of the mass, rather than for the aggrandizement of the individual, the Bahais anticipate that national and economic affairs will be so regulated that comparatively little misery will exist in the world. There will not be the extremes of wealth and poverty which now exist and all people, both rich and poor, will be better off than now.

Through the stable financial conditions which co-operation between capital and labor will bring about (co-operation for the best good of all concerned), the laborer will be assured of a livelihood and will be enabled to get the best out of life, and, upon the other hand, the capitalist will be less on the defensive and less burdened than he is now. Because of the co-operation of all classes, the wealthy will occupy themselves more with matters pertaining to the general welfare of the people, rather than seeking mainly their own individual enjoyment.

As people come into the spirit of the Bahai teaching and see the virtue of co-operation, and act upon this principle, the great economic problems which now threaten the world with dire calamities will disappear and give place to institutions for the highest good of mankind, through which all people will live in harmony, in happiness and in plenty. The Bahais believe that eventually the whole world will recognize the power of the spiritual principle of co-operation, and will apply it in matters of every day life, thus solving life's mighty economic problem in all of its details.

XVII.
THE EVOLUTION OF MAN.

The Bahais teach the existence of five kingdoms, planes, divisions or kinds of creation:

(1) The mineral kingdom, or material plane in which there is no life or spirit, in the ordinary acceptance of the term.

(2) The vegetable kingdom or physical plane, in which there is the lowest form of spirit or life. This plane is characterized by the principle of growth and fruition, by virtue of which organisms develop and propagate their kind.

(3) The animal kingdom or psychical plane, the organisms of which are differentiated from those of the vegetable plane by the power to apprehend conditions outside of themselves.

(4) The human kingdom, that of man, which is differentiated from the animal condition by the intellectual faculty, by virtue of which man comprehends ideas in the abstract.

(5) The divine kingdom, or condition of spiritual illumination, which is differentiated from the human, or natural, or unspiritually quickened state of the soul, by consciousness of God. By virtue of this higher life, the quickened soul apprehends spiritual realities, lives in spiritual communion with the divine, and is of the order of The Kingdom of God. Unlike the vegetable, animal and human kingdoms, which are dependent for existence upon earthly conditions, the spiritual life of the soul is dependent upon those peculiar to the divine realm. These conditions are eternal, therefore the life of divinely quickened souls is eternal. The spiritual condition in which those souls live is not confined to an earthly realm.

Beyond and above all created kind is the Holy

Spirit of God, uncreated and infinite, unknowable to man save through Its Manifestation, the mediator between God and His children here upon earth. Divinely quickened man is the highest of the creatures, above which there is no creation. From his beginning man was created man—a distinct species. In the early days of man upon earth, in many respects he more resembled the animal than he did the man type of today. But from his first appearance there was in him that human spirit, apart and of a different kind from the animal, which, though at first hidden, has evolved into the type of man that we now know. In the coming age of divine development, humanity will continue evolving to a far higher state than it now has attained. Man, never having been anything but man, can never evolve out of the kingdom of his own kind and species. He will, however, be approaching nearer and nearer to the perfect type of *spiritual* manhood and perfection.

XVIII.
THE METHOD OF TEACHING AND THE GROWTH OF THE BAHAI MOVEMENT.

The method of Bahai teaching is constructive, in every sense. In presenting this cause to a soul, the teacher's first step is to confirm the seeker in the truth of his own religion, and upon that, as a foundation, place this latter-day teaching. Argument and dispute have no place in this cause. The teaching is quietly yet fearlessly given, and then the matter is left with the listener and God. People are not urged or enticed, but rather, through love, are attracted to the cause.

It has been found, when two or more souls come together to discuss religious matters with perfect love in their hearts, the result is always uplifting and conducive to edification. When people meet together for religious discussion without this spirit of true charity in their hearts, the result is always distressing, and it would have been better had they not met. This principle of the power of love the Bahais understand, and they rely upon it and not upon arguments presented from the plane of intellect alone.

In order to combat evil the soul should be filled with love and truth. Fear, together with all its attending destructive forces, disappears in the presence of faith and assurance. *The Bahai teaching is one of joy and gladness.* True spirituality is profound yet not depressing, and while uplifting, is free from levity. Truth and love are in the world to lift people up from suffering and depression, and should, therefore, be presented as they are, full of joy. The Bahais are taught at all times to manifest in their thoughts, words and actions the joy of the Lord. It is only by showing forth a joyful and happy spirit, and by loving service to humanity, that suffering and seeking souls are attracted and brought under the power of the quickening spirit of the cause. Through kind and loving service to all humanity, to friend and foe alike, the Bahais have a most powerful weapon with which to combat religious prejudice and spiritual ignorance. Even the most difficult people are won through continued kindness. Once attracted, the hungry soul recognizes and accepts the Truth. The Bahai teachers find that when a soul is reached by their teaching, whether a Christian, Moslem, Jew or Buddhist, the truth at once appeals to his inner nature, and he will usually say, "This is exactly what I have always believed".

Having no organization, ritual, or priesthood after the manner of other religions, the Bahais are opposing the work of no other religious bodies. It is a world-wide movement, the spirit of which is working unhindered and unbound by confines and barriers of sect and ism. The Bahais see and recognize truth and spiritual beauty wherever found, and through this attitude of love and tolerance for all, they find at every hand, among the people of other religious bodies, the opportunity of sharing the spirit of their faith.

Often people inquire whether affiliation with the Bahai cause necessitates the giving up of church membership. The advice is always that no human or religious relations should be severed, but that these relations should become as avenues for giving forth the message and the spirit of the Bahai faith. People having church relations continue to mingle with church people. However, they do not remain silent about the new light which has come to them. When ever they find prepared souls, they give them the glad tidings of the coming of The Lord in His Kingdom, and thus they diffuse the knowledge and spirit of the Truth.

Where there are several sympathizers in the work in the same vicinity, regular meetings are established. At these reunions the sacred writings are read, the teachings are explained, and seekers are welcomed. As these groups increase in numbers, they become known as "Assemblies." In the assemblies certain people are usually selected to serve. These confer together and arrange for meetings, publications, and other matters in connection with the carrying on of the work.

There is no distinction such as teacher or pupil. All are teachers and at the same time all are pupils. Contributions are not solicited. The cause must first find root in the hearts of the people, then the people will of themselves arise to serve it. When a soul realizes the greatness of the privilege of aiding the Bahai work, then he assists, in the measure in which he is able, his own heart being his guide.

The Bahais are working toward the great end of uniting all races and religions in the Love of the Lord. They are impelled by no other motive than the Love of God. They are not looking for results, theirs is the satisfaction of service, and there is no other satisfaction or pleasure which can approach that joy, the joy of serving God.

One of the questions the Bahais are often asked, is regarding the number of those who profess this faith. The reason for their inability to answer is quite clear to those who realize that the object of this movement is to leaven the whole lump of humanity, with its numerous divisions, rather than to precipitate another sect upon the many already existent. Having no form of membership, the Bahais make no attempt to estimate their number. Their strength is a spiritual strength, not to be measured numerically. Even were it possible to know the exact number of Bahais in the world, this reckoning would be of short duration because the movement is growing continually, interest in it is increasing, and the hearts of people are daily becoming more attracted, and more confirmed in the truth.

The Bahais are widely distributed throughout the world. During the days of The Bab, His cause was confined principally to Persia, though He had adherents also in Turkey and in neighboring countries. With the rise of Baha-'o'llah, this field of work was extended. The Bahai teachers went north into Caucasia, Russia and Turkestan, south into India, east into Burma and later on into China. With Baha-'o'llah's exile in Turkey, Roumelia and Syria, His cause spread in those countries as well as in Egypt and in Arabia.

The establishment of the Bahai cause in the West has been accomplished under the ministry of Abdul-Baha. In the year 1894, a small group of people in the city of Chicago became interested in the Revelation. Later, similar groups were formed in New York, Washington, and San Francisco. In the winter of 1898-99, the first band of American Bahai pilgrims crossed the seas to visit Abdul-Baha, then in exile in the Holy Land. Up to that time the communication between the American Bahais and Abdul-Baha had been by writing only. Then, with the added impetus of Abdul-Baha's personal touch, these American pilgrims returned to the West with renewed zeal and desire to spread the cause,

From the enthusiasm of this first band of travelers, new centers of the teaching were founded in France, England and America. From these as a nucleus have developed Believers, in all parts of the United States, in Canada, Mexico, Hawaii, Japan and Australia, as well as in various parts of Germany, Switzerland and Italy. During this period of growth, several Bahai teachers from the Orient have traveled through Europe and America, instructing and teaching the people and helping to establish new centers. Likewise, teachers from the Occident have traveled and taught in the oriental countries. Quietly and slowly the cause has grown amid all varieties of human conditions, among peoples of every religion, race and clime. In the growth and progress of the Bahai Movement is demonstrated its universal spiritual power. Accepted by people of every condition, it is making inroads into their souls, as leaven; it is uniting these many heterogeneous elements into one homogeneous world-people.

XIX.
A PERSONAL TESTIMONY

In the preceding chapters of this book I have attempted to give a general resumé of the history and teaching of the Bahai cause, and the work now being accomplished. Here it is my desire to relate to the reader a few of my *own* experiences in connection with this cause. During the past twelve years, it has been my privilege to visit Abdul-Baha several times and to travel extensively among the Bahais in foreign lands. It is with the desire of sharing the inspiration received from Abdul-Baha and from his followers, that I am presuming to record these personal observations.

My first visit to Abdul-Baha was in the winter of 1901. At that time the cause in the West was in its infancy and was passing through a critical period of its growth. But few of the words of Baha'o'llah and Abdul-Baha had been translated, and the believers, though fired with faith and a great desire to disseminate the teachings had as yet, learned but little of the spiritual principles of the cause. Consequently there was a general lack of harmony of ideas among the adherents, which caused much confusion. It was against such odds that Abdul-Baha was heroically struggling.

At that time he was in comparative ease, having been allowed to leave the prison city of Akka with its unhealthy climate, and was spending the winter in the neighboring town of Haifa. Notwithstanding this betterment in the conditions of Abdul-Baha's outer life, one felt the weight which was upon his soul and saw how his spirit was taxed in his endeavor to teach and train the people in the way of The Kingdom.

I recall an incident which showed the stress under which he, at that time, was laboring. One night after a busy day of teaching and letter writing he had gathered twenty or more of us at his table for the late evening meal. We were about half through with the repast, when some one made an allusion to some difficulty among the believers in America. Abdul-Baha looked very serious, then in evident distress of both mind and body he arose from the table and left the room. As he went through the door his aba (cloak) fell from his shoulders to the floor. Gathering it up I hurriedly followed him to the terrace in front of the house. Scarcely touching him I slipped the cloak over his shoulders. He did not notice the incident, so troubled and absorbed was he as he passed out into the night.

For over a year before I first met Abdul-Baha, I had been a believer in the Bahai cause, so when I went to him it was not to have my faith established but rather to have it confirmed, and to gain knowledge. In the accomplishment of this, Abdul-Baha helped through his understanding of me. From the moment I met him I realized he understood me perfectly, as an old friend. Thus a bond was established, which has always been a source of joy, delight, and help to me, for each visit I have had with him, and every tablet (letter) and message received from him, has strengthened this understanding and has demonstrated to me again and again, Abdul-Baha's all-penetrating spiritual sight and wisdom. Notwithstanding the distance and circumstances which separate Abdul-Baha from his friends, when they receive his tablets they find advices and admonitions peculiarly applicable to them in their needs of that moment.

During the eleven days I remained in Haifa,

I had this phase of Abdul-Baha's personality deeply engraved on my mind. All was not easy to understand. I had various spiritual ups and downs until shortly before I left him, then everything became very clear and my spiritual rapport with him was established. The moment of our parting was a happy one for me, because I felt that I was carrying away with me something which could never be destroyed, a spiritual friendship which would grow eternally, both here and in the future realm.

Early in the summer of 1901, shortly after my first visit, an order was issued sending Abdul-Baha back to the prison city of Akka. There he remained for seven years, with the exception of a short period, when upon several occasions he was permitted to visit the tomb of Baha'o'llah at Behjé, a mile or two beyond the city gates. During this period of imprisonment, it was at times with the utmost difficulty that pilgrims were able to see Abdul-Baha, nevertheless this was a great period of growth in the cause. Abdul-Baha worked diligently with his pen and the result of his labors became apparent among the Bahais in all parts of the world.

Six years elapsed between my first and second visits to Abdul-Baha, during which interim he had been confined to the fortress. Knowing that some recent pilgrims had remained nine days in Akka, I had rather set my mind upon a visit of the same length. On reaching Haifa I was told that, on account of the troublous conditions surrounding Abdul-Baha, I would be able to remain with him but a few hours. At first the thought of so short a visit was a keen disappointment. Upon second thought, however, my mental attitude changed and I realized fully that Abdul-Baha understood and was planning for the best.

Whether one is benefitted by meeting Abdul-Baha depends upon really *meeting him spiritually*. It is the open, unprejudiced and seeking souls which unite with the soul of Abdul-Baha. When this spiritual contact is effected, the personal visit to him is not essential for enlightenment, for, with spiritual connection between the souls of Abdul-Baha (the heart of the Bahai movement) and the believers (the members of the body of the movement), these souls are one with him, and through this unity his divine wisdom and love go forth to all his followers.

Although my second visit with Abdul-Baha was very short, I would not have wished it otherwise. Again I left him in great joy with my soul overflowing with the love of The Kingdom, which he so freely radiates. The one great lesson which he taught me at that time was dispelling (negative) fear with (positive) assurance.

The natural tendency of man is often to fear people and to shut himself away from them. This becomes a habit and one which causes much ill ease, and this condition I was just beginning to realize. Not from anything which Abdul-Baha said to me, but through the way in which he received and treated me I saw clearly that I could not serve him in the cause and continue to remain inwardly aloof from people. I saw that it was because of Abdul-Baha's freedom from constraint, and through his fearlessness and his friendly way of approaching people, his frank expression of love, faith and assurance, that he was able to reach the souls of men and impart to them his courage and wisdom.

Abdul-Baha throws himself into the lives of

all about him. Through this contact he undoubtedly suffers much, nevertheless, thus he is enabled to reach the people and to minister to them. His fearlessness, combined with gentleness and humility in approaching people, was a lesson to me, for in his method I saw the way in which Abdul-Baha's followers must live in order to do his work among men.

My next visit to Abdul-Baha was at the culmination of his troubles and difficulties just previous to the fall of the former despotic Ottoman power, and the re-establishment of the constitutional government in the midsummer of 1908. Upon arriving in Haifa, I found that some recent American pilgrims had not been able to meet Abdul-Baha, but had returned to America happy in having seen him from a distance as he walked upon an elevated balcony on his house within the fortifications of Akka. Four Arabs, recent converts to the faith, on account of their belief had for several months been confined in the prison of the fortress. Others of the Bahais, in order to avoid pending trouble, by Abdul-Baha's advice had sought temporary refuge in Egypt, while those remaining in Syria were all but panic stricken by the trouble and persecutions which were daily descending upon the Bahai community from the hands of the unscrupulous government officials.

After remaining several days in Haifa, word came from Abdul-Baha for me to go to Akka and proceed to the house of a certain Persian gentleman, one of the oldest and most faithful of the believers. In the guise of a native Syrian and with the assistance of one of the oriental Bahais, I entered the prison city, passing through the various guarded gates without being halted. Once established in the privacy of the house of the friend, Abdul-Baha having the freedom of the city within the fortifications, came to see me several times.

Though under the most severe physical difficulties, Abdul-Baha was visibly in the greatest spiritual strength and power. In strong contrast with the fear and terror of his followers, impossible to describe, Abdul-Baha stood forth in the greatest of joy of soul and tranquility of spirit. He radiated calmness and assurance, and through his strength the community of the friends was saved from despair and from the disaster which would have accompanied the loss of hope at such a moment. This situation was dramatic in the extreme. It was shortly followed by the tragic downfall of the government that for forty years had held Abdul-Baha a prisoner.

Several months later I was again permitted to travel in Syria and visit Abdul-Baha. Although it had not been long in point of time since my previous visit, yet the conditions surrounding Abdul-Baha had so changed as to make the previous time seem, by comparison, to have been in a former decade. Abdul-Baha was free. The uttermost liberty existed. Akka had ceased to be a penal colony and the gates were no longer guarded.

The Bahais had not yet recovered from their first ecstasy of joy over the freedom of Abdul-Baha, yet through all this manifest jubilation he was conducting his work as usual. It was then that I realized, to the extent of my capacity, how far above this world's conditions Abdul-Baha stands. Not discouraged by criticism, persecution, calamity; not elated by applause, commendation nor good fortune, he stands apart from the world upon a firm rock, the spiritual foundation of The Kingdom. By virtue of this severance from all save God, he is enabled to change the current of the world's thought from materiality to spirituality, and to create in men's souls the fire of God's love.

Almost two years after the great change in Turkey, I again went to Syria. In coming in contact with Abdul-Baha each soul receives the message, or the lesson, for which it is then ready and prepared to receive. Previously my attention had been chiefly called to those principles for which Abdul-Baha stands, which are so clearly manifested in his life, while his personality, as a man in the world, had impressed me but little. Now, this which previously I had allowed to pass almost unnoticed was to be my chief lesson.

I saw the exquisite beauty of Abdul-Baha's personality from lines of physical strength and refinement in his face, to his trained thought and judgment. His dignity and carriage, his mental grasp of things both great and small, and the manner in which he dealt with them in proportion to their importance, were all of the deepest interest to me.

In his person one sees at once the power of the spirit as well as its gentle, refining qualities, a combination of strength and delicacy, of masculine and feminine qualities; the balanced combination of dignity, humility, forcefulness and gentleness.

Whatever may be one's mental conception of Abdul-Baha, one must invariably readjust it from time to time. Under his guidance, his followers are growing in spiritual stature, and as the perceptive powers of the soul increase, one sees more and more clearly Abdul-Baha's spiritual power and divine mission. Were one to visit him many times, each time his former idea would be laid aside for a clearer and a more defined conception.

My last visit with Abdul-Baha was in September, 1911, during his sojourn in London, England. There he was in the vortex of western civilization, sought by many people from various walks of life, both high and low. Under these conditions his spirit shone forth with greater brilliancy than ever before.

It is natural and easy for the western mind to weave a halo of sentiment and romance about the personality of a persecuted religious leader, exiled and imprisoned for his faith under the corrupt rule of an oriental despot; but, when this same spiritual teacher comes into the limelight of western thought and customs, the people see him from a different angle; things which they but imagined about him are dispelled, and his real virtues stand out more strikingly visible than ever.

Abdul-Baha, stripped of his accustomed oriental environment, appeared more clearly than ever to be the master of the *spiritual* situation. I heard him give the first public address that he had ever made, before a vast concourse of about 2,000 souls, and I was also with him during a number of personal interviews granted to various truth seekers. At all times under these unaccustomed conditions he drew unto himself all people, and through his love, wisdom and power, gave them spiritual assurance and satisfaction.

One afternoon some one asked Abdul-Baha regarding the relation of his mission to that of the great Manifestation, Baha'o'llah. He replied by saying, "Baha'o'llah is the root of the tree of The Kingdom, while I am the branch, branched from that pre-existent root. The fruit of the tree appears upon the branches, not upon the roots."

The most potent of all factors in moving humanity is *love;* it is at the same time the most elusive and the most difficult of all things to define. We know it only through its characteristics, and these we never fail to recognize. So it is with *true religion.* There is a spiritual force, which is *divine love,* working in it that is its very life force. When one feels his soul responding to this, he realizes that he has come into contact with a higher realm, and though he cannot describe this awakening in so many words, it is none the less to him the most real of all things.

In these latter days, when "prophets" and "new religions" are so abundant, one naturally wonders how to distinguish truth from error, and how to recognize the Lord's anointed one from among many men. The difficulty was solved almost two thousand years ago by him who said, "By their fruits ye shall know them".

To him who has traveled and lived among the Bahais and has seen the effect of this cause upon the lives of peoples of every race and religion, there can be no doubt as to the divine source of its teachings, for in the fruits of the Bahai cause is manifest its truth.

It has been my privilege to travel among, and to associate with, the Bahais in many foreign countries, and I can testify to the spiritual qualities manifested in their lives. Often I have been in a position where I have been obliged to place myself entirely in the hands of strange men, whose language I could not speak, the only thing which we had in common being our faith. I say the *only thing* was our faith, yet this was everything because that faith was large enough to encompass all things.

Western travelers whom I have met in the oriental countries have been surprised that I trusted myself in out-of-the-way places and along unfrequented routes of travel, alone with the oriental people as my sole companions and friends. When one is surrounded by friends, his personal welfare is seldom a subject of worry. I can truthfully state that never have I felt more at ease and free from care than when I have been with the oriental Bahais. Wherever I happened to be with them, I have always had a warmth of hospitality and kindness lavished upon me. This was not because of any other reason than that I was of their faith.

Between the Bahais of the East and those of the West there exists the strongest tie. Since it was through the suffering, pain, and trials of the Bahais of the Orient that this faith had its first growth and was brought to the West, the western Bahais look toward their eastern brothers and sisters with deepest feelings of love and gratitude. Western Bahais have in their souls a strong love for the eastern Bahais and a burning desire to go to them sharing with them all the practical things of the western civilization.

Upon the other hand, in the growth of the Bahai cause here in the West the oriental Bahais see the result of their labors, for these believers are their spiritual offspring. They see the fruit of their bloody persecution and great sufferings, and with open and joyful hearts they are anxious to receive into their very lives their western brothers and sisters, learning from them and in turn pouring out upon them, all of that wealth of devotion, love, and spiritual assurance, which the people of the East have and which the people of the West need.

Among the Bahais there is a practical demonstration of a combined religious and secular unity. Good works are not done under the name of *"charity"* nor *"philanthropy"*. Rather, it is *"reciprocation"* and *"interdependence"*. Each gives what he has to give, and through the spirit of giving and doing in loving service, ones own nature unfolds and he himself receives abundantly.

Particularly in the Orient the contrast between the Bahais and other people is very striking. There, the average Orientals and Occidentals, meet without mingling, each remaining foreign to the other, but the opposite is true with these very same people when they are touched by the Bahai spirit, for then we see them associating with one another as members of one family, having the same interests and desires, and united in the same works.

Among the oriental Bahais there is a love and a devotion to this cause and its principles, impossible to describe. It is beyond comprehension to understand, yet one recognizes it.

In many countries and among people of every race and of every religion I found such a warm welcome and had such friendship and devotion showered upon me, simply because I was a Bahai, that I felt and saw the blending process at work, uniting the East and the West. This is a force working independently of material conditions. I saw it working under all conditions and amid all surroundings, from those of the half-naked jungleman living in his hut, to those of the cultured man of wealth dwelling in his palace. This spiritual love, which is of God, is the strongest power in creation. In its uniting force is the foundation of accord and harmony upon which the Orient and the Occident are meeting. From this movement will appear, as fruits, all of those social institutions between the East and the West, which will materially demonstrate the truths which the Bahais now witness as spiritual realities.

In Persia I found the Bahais struggling against great opposition upon the part of those surrounding them, in their work of uplifting and educating woman. While in that country, I met Bahai women who are doing great work for their own sex. Until recently this work, for the most part, has been very quietly done, in fact almost in secret, on account of the persecution by the Moslems, whose traditions regarding the seclusion and oppression of women, the Bahais are undermining.

I found the Persian believers to be most stanch and courageous people. While the great massacres and martyrdoms of the Bahais in that land are probably now a thing of the past, nevertheless the Bahais are still under persecution and even in these days it sometimes leads to loss of life.

Many men whom I met had been eyewitnesses to the massacres of the 80's, in which so many of our people died for their faith, while others with whom I talked had lost both family and property. One impression which I recall very vividly, was the calm way, free from any trace of rancor, in which the Persian Bahais referred to the losses and afflictions visited upon them by the enemies of the cause. Instead of causing embitterment, these troubles have had a most spiritualizing effect upon the believers, for the persecution has been as a fire which has taken everything from them save the love of God, with which their hearts are ablaze.

After a visit among these people, one

feels spiritually better and stronger than before, absorbing a force from them which gives courage in moments of weakness and guidance in moments of strength. This is the spirit which abides with those who are in reality severed from all save God. It is this spirit which is manifest in the life and teaching of Abdul-Baha, and in the lives of those who in spirit follow the principles for which he stands.

www.ingramcontent.com/pod-product-compliance
Lightning Source LLC
Chambersburg PA
CBHW061330040426
42444CB00011B/2850

* 9 7 8 1 6 3 3 9 1 5 9 0 9 *